The SECRET LIFE *of an Arable*
FIELD
PLANTS, ANIMALS AND THE ECOSYSTEM

To my brothers, Charlie and James

And the happy days we had running through the cornfields together as children

The SECRET LIFE *of an Arable* FIELD

PLANTS, ANIMALS AND THE ECOSYSTEM

Sophie McCallum

WHITE OWL

AN IMPRINT OF PEN & SWORD BOOKS LTD.
YORKSHIRE – PHILADELPHIA

First published in Great Britain in 2021 by
Pen and Sword WHITE OWL
An imprint of
Pen & Sword Books Ltd
Yorkshire - Philadelphia

ISBN 978 1 52678 844 3

Typeset in 11/14 pts Cormorant Infant
by SJmagic DESIGN SERVICES, India.

Printed and bound in India by Replika Press Pvt. Ltd.

Pen & Sword Books Ltd incorporates the imprints of Pen & Sword Books Archaeology, Atlas, Aviation, Battleground, Discovery, Family History, History, Maritime, Military, Naval, Politics, Railways, Select, Transport, True Crime, Fiction, Frontline Books, Leo Cooper, Praetorian Press, Seaforth Publishing, Wharncliffe and White Owl.

For a complete list of Pen & Sword titles please contact

PEN & SWORD BOOKS LIMITED
47 Church Street, Barnsley, South Yorkshire, S70 2AS, England
E-mail: enquiries@pen-and-sword.co.uk
Website: www.pen-and-sword.co.uk

or

PEN AND SWORD BOOKS
1950 Lawrence Rd, Havertown, PA 19083, USA
E-mail: Uspen-and-sword@casematepublishers.com
Website: www.penandswordbooks.com

Contents

First there is food. Agriculture in the UK is a £5.3 billion industry, employing 1.5% of the workforce – that is 476,000 people, using 69% of the landmass. There are 212,000 farm holdings covering 23.07 million acres. One third of this is arable land, with the remainder being grassland. The UK is only capable of generating 60% of its total food intake, although this would be greater if we ate seasonally.

65% of all cereal crops are wheat. 31 million sheep graze the country, as well as 10 million cattle, 9.6 million poultry and 4.5 million pigs.

The average age of a farmer in the UK is 60 years old.

95% of pesticides used affect non-target species. Unfortunately, the full impact of pesticides on soil micro-organisms is not entirely understood. Runoff takes them into waterways, and wind carries them to unintentioned environments. Pests mutate genetically to become resistant over time, with chemicals entering the food chain, creating the deaths of birds and fish, and eventually humans. In the UK, populations of 10 bird species fell by 10 million in the 20 years from 1979, with the US losing 72 million birds annually due to pesticides. Humans suffer from birth defects, tumours, blood and nerve disorders, coma and even death as a result of pesticide poisoning. DDT reduces male penis size in embryonic mammals and leads to undescended testicles. The loss of pests causes an outbreak in populations of their prey, resulting in further expensive crop damage.

Under the Countryside Stewardship scheme, the UK government is paying for farmers to support wildlife, by providing sources of nectar and pollen for insect pollinators, supplying winter food for seed-eating birds and improving habitats for both.

Now that there is a planning permission proposal to build on the fields where I live, I feel really sad about the rich flora and fauna that we will all miss. I have seen a badger feeding there, twice in two days, while a fox darted out yesterday close by across the path. It is a photographer's delight, where you can capture the light on the cow parsley and poppies in the evening sun. The woodland path where I walk is an ancient one, used by cattle going to market in times gone by.

This book details 120 species of insect, butterfly and moth, animal, crop, wildflower, tree and bird that all inhabit and interact in the arable land ecosystem. They are invaluable in ways which we are only just beginning to understand. Across the EU, 84% of crops, with a value of £12.6 billion are pollinated by insects. This is a free service, and not one to be taken lightly.

Adder

The adder, *Vipera berus*, goes by many names, partially due to the fact that its range is enormous – spreading from western Europe right into east Asia. This common European adder can also be known as the common viper, crossed viper, common crossed adder or variations on this theme. Although its bite can be extremely painful, death is rare. They are not aggressive by nature and will only lash out if provoked, stepped on, or picked up.

The adder is ovoviviparous, meaning that its young are encased in an egg, which hatches before birth within the body of the parent. This is opposed to oviparous, where the young are produced from the egg after it has been laid by the parent, such as with chickens. Alternatively, viviparous is when the parent delivers a live young, which it has developed within its own body, as do humans.

Adult length is in the region of 60 to 90cm, and they weigh 50 to 180g. Size will vary geographically, with adders of 104cm being seen in Scandinavia.

Snakes do not have a good write up historically, starting with the *Book of Genesis*. The adder itself takes its name from the Old English word for serpent, 'nœdre', which has German roots.

Colouration of the adder varies from snake to snake. Some will be a very pale fawn, exhibiting darker dorsal crossbars. Others will be a deeper shade of brown, with distinct, black markings. There are even some melanistic individuals, which are very dark, showing no dorsal markings whatsoever. Commonly, a dorsal zigzag pattern is seen, running the entire length of the body. There is predominantly a dark 'X' or 'V' on the head, with a dark streak running from the corner of the eye, through the neck, breaking up to a series of spots along the side of the body. There is slight sexual dimorphism, which is not usually seen in snakes – females are usually brown, with darker brown markings, and males tend to be grey with black patterning.

There are four snake species in the UK. Only the adder is harmful. The other three – the grass snake, barred grass snake and the smooth snake – are not dangerous.

The adder needs a varied habitat in order to fulfil its needs of basking, foraging and hibernation. Predation and human contact also have to be fitted into the equation. In reality, it likes meadows, woodland extremities, hedgerows and scrubby hills, chalk downs, rocks, moors and heaths, coastal dunes, quarries and even rubbish tips. As long as there is dry ground within reach, it will also inhabit wetland areas. They could be anywhere!

The adder is protected under UK law. The Wildlife and Countryside Act of 1981 says that it is illegal to kill, injure, harm or sell the adder. Norway and Denmark passed similar laws in the same year. The adder is listed under Appendix III of the Berne Convention, protecting the species and its habitat. However, the International Union for Conservation of Nature (IUCN), although recognising habitat destruction, feels that due to its wide distribution, the species is of 'least concern'. The adder is poached for sale in the pet trade. The snakes are also taken to remove their venom, in a process known as 'milking', to create anti-venom that can save the lives of people with a snakebite.

Adders are diurnal, meaning they are only active during the day, although the further south you go in its range, the more the adder is awake in the evenings and even night during the summer months. Although an earth dwelling creature, it can climb banks and small bushes to catch the sun's rays or if it senses prey.

Adders are frightened by humans, removing themselves from the vicinity if they sense their presence. They will bite only when provoked, and will warn off potential predation by hissing loudly and raising their front body into an 'S' shape in order to attack. Pregnant females give off the most warning.

Adders spend their winters in hibernation. In the UK this amounts to 150 days for males and 180 days for females. In the northernmost parts of their range, e.g. Sweden, this is extended to eight to nine months. Hibernation is not without its risks and a large proportion of snakes will die – approximately 15% of adults and 30 to 40% of young. The snakes may make the most of warmer winter days by coming out to bask in the sun.

ADDER

The adder preys on moles, voles, shrews, lizards and slow worms, and if it is looking for a feast it can take weasels and rats. Frogs and other amphibians are also at risk. Birds, eggs and young are taken, with the adder climbing up to reach its prey. Diet varies according to location. Young adders have a similar diet to adults, also eating worms and spiders, and they will stabilise on the adult diet when they have reached 30cm in length.

Mating has been seen from June to early October. Males follow the female's scent trail. They exhibit a side-to-side parallel 'flowing' flirtation, where they flick their tongues over each other's bodies and whip their tails. They remain with each other for a few days after mating. The male may have to fight off competitors. He will exhibit the 'adder dance' whilst doing this, whereby the two males will raise their bodies and fight to bring the other to the ground. This will carry on until one is exhausted and retreats. Usually the male who has just mated wins this battle, as his chemistry has been focused by copulation. They do not bite one another during this ritual.

Young are born in August to September, sometimes a month earlier or a month later. There are 3 to 20 in each litter, and they are contained in a see-through sac from which they must emerge. Most adders manage to achieve this whilst still in their mother's body. They are 14 to 23cm in length and are able to give a dangerous snake bite from birth. Mothers are not particularly maternal. The young will stay with her for only a few days.

There are eight anti-venoms on the market for the adder, with livestock and domestic animals also at risk. In the UK, the months of March to October carry the highest threat. Sweden suffers roughly 1,300 bites a year, of which 12% need hospital treatment. In the UK there have been 14 deaths since 1876. Children are most at risk. A doctor should be consulted immediately after a bite. Recovery rates differ, but can take up to 12 months. There will be localised pain, followed by swelling. Tenderness and inflammation occur throughout the limb and may spread, especially in a child, throughout the whole body. An anaphylaxis reaction can occur.

Alder

The alder belongs to the genus *Alnus*: flowering plants in the birch family, Betulaceae. In this genus there are around 35 monoecious species, i.e. containing both male and female reproductive organs on the same individual tree or shrub.

The species that we are looking at is the common alder, or *Alnus glutinosa*, native to most of Europe, southwest Asia and north Africa. Pollen grains found in peat wetland inform us that the alder has been in Britain for at least 8,000 years. It has suffered from the drainage of farming fields as it thrives in wet ground. It prefers a pH of 5.5 to 7.2.

Similar to members of the pea family, the alder roots incorporate a nitrogen-fixing bacterium (*Frankia alni*) with which it has a vital symbiotic relationship. The bacterium is found in the alder's root nodules, sometimes growing as large as a fist. This bacterium takes in nitrogen from the surrounding soil, providing it to the tree. The alder, in return, gives the bacterium sugars, which it forms during photosynthesis. This increases the fertility of the soil and allows other species to grow. In this respect, alder is seen as a pioneer species, allowing for the development of successional species.

Alder is used to enrich poor ground, as well as preventing the erosion of river banks. By getting the eco-system ball rolling, the alder will eventually die out in woodlands through loss of light to seedlings as they grow larger.

The tree is a source of nourishment and shelter to wildlife, with a range of insects, fungi and lichen relying solely on this tree. The seeds are valuable to birds in winter, and rabbits, hares, deer, sheep and other livestock shelter and feed from the tree. The root system is beneficial to fish sheltering during flooding as well as providing important shade. Over 140 insects are known to feed from the alder. Lichens enjoy the moist atmosphere of the tree when it is growing near water. As well as *Frankia alni*, 46 other species of symbiotic fungi make use of the alder, many of which are specialised to this tree.

Alders will grow to 20 to 30 metres, sometimes even higher. They exhibit a smooth, glossy bark whilst young, growing to a dark grey, fissured texture in older trees. Leaves have a short stalk and they stay on the tree longer if growing near water, staying green well into the autumn. Buds and young leaves are sticky with a resinous gum, hence the Latin name *glutinosa*, which means 'sticky', particularly in respect to young shoots. Catkins appear in autumn, both male and female varieties on the same tree. The male catkins are reddish, and hang down 5 to 10cm from the tree. The female catkins are upright, and green with short stalks. They will turn dark brown and woody over the autumn. Catkins are dormant throughout the winter and are pollinated by the wind in spring. The female seeds are winged, which allows them to stay in the air for longer, increasing their coverage. Seeds are also dispersed by water.

The tree lives to around 160 years, but heart rot tends to set in, so they are usually felled at 60 to 70 years. They can be coppiced. Some countries, for example New Zealand, consider this introduced species a weed. It pushes out native plants and affects the nutrient level in the soil.

However, the alder is useful. When cut it is white, before turning a pale red with attractive knots. It is widely used in papermaking and fibreboard. Due to its strength and longevity underwater, it has been used in building the deep foundations of Venice and those of many medieval cathedrals. Alder can be used in joinery, for both timber and veneer. It is also utilised in woodturning and carving, as well as for furniture and window frames, and is soft and light enough for clogs, broom handles, toys, pencils and bowls.

As the bark and twigs of alder are made up of 17 to 20% tannic acid, they have found a use over the years in tanning and dying. However, they do create a very strong colour in the tanning process, which defines their use. Dyeing creates various shades of brown, beige, yellow and orange depending on the fixative and methods used, and they colour a range of fabrics from wool to cotton and silk. The bark, fruit and leaves are all used in the dyeing process. The wood is used to smoke fish. It also produces a good charcoal. Due to the sticky nature of the leaves, they have been spread on floors to trap fleas and other insects.

THE SECRET LIFE OF AN ARABLE FIELD

Ants

There are relatively few ants in the UK. Their population is determined by soil temperature, resulting in the south of England having the greatest diversity and number of species. They live in a range of habitats, varying from heathland to wooded areas, where they live in leaf litter, or under stones and logs. Different subfamilies, for example *Dolichoderinae* and *Formicinae*, exhibit different anatomies.

Ant fossils embedded in amber have been found in Myanmar, suggesting that ants originated over 140 million years ago during the Cretaceous period. Flowering plants developed at about the same time, leading to diversification within ant species. During the Cretaceous period ants only made up 1% of insect numbers and were based mainly in the northern hemisphere. They evolved to fill different

ecological niches at the start of the Paleogene period, starting 66 million years ago, becoming a more dominant organism, so that by the Oligocene and Miocene periods, 33 and 23 million years ago respectively, they formed between 20 and 40% of all insect fossils.

Ants developed from wasp-like species and belong to the order Hymenoptera, similar to sawflies, wasps and bees, although ants are in the Formicidae family. There are thought to be 22,000 different species, of which over 12,500 have been recorded. Their identifying features of jointed antennae and the characteristic node-like structure that defines their tiny waist makes them simple to recognise.

They are eusocial insects, meaning they have a high level of organisation within their society, shown by co-operative brood care, overlapping generations of adults within the group and the splitting of work between breeding and non-breeding groups.

Ant colonies can be as small as 50 individuals up to vast colonies numbering millions. These larger groups are made up of sterile, wingless worker ants and soldiers, both of which are female, as well as fertile males known as 'drones', and at least one fertile female, called the 'queen'. They labour collaboratively to support the group. They are able to solve complex problems, where they utilise division of labour and communication between individuals.

Ants are very successful. They have spread throughout the world, with the exception of Antarctica and a few islands such as Greenland, Iceland and areas of Polynesia. Ants are thought to make up 15 to 25% of all land-living animal biomass, extending to 25% in the tropics. This is more than vertebrates – a sign of their ecological dominance. Most ant species are generalists, feeding on plants or animals, whilst a few are specialist feeders. They populate a large variety of ecological niches. Some species of ant are used as biological pest control agents.

Africa hosts the largest number of ant species, with 2,500 recorded. The Neotropics in central and south America follow a close second with 2,162, and Asia has 2,080 species. By contrast, Europe has only 180 classified ant species. This shows how most ants prefer a higher temperature to flourish.

Ants vary in size from a tiny 0.75mm to 52mm. They are usually red or black, but can also be seen in green or with a metallic sheen in the tropics. As they are so easy to spot and study they become a useful animal to gauge the health of an eco-system.

Ants differ from other insects as they have elbowed antennae, unique secretory glands, and a narrowing of their second stomach region to form a waist. Similar to other insects, they have an exoskeleton which protects the whole of their body and gives a place for muscles to attach. They lack lungs; instead respiratory gases travel through their exoskeleton using miniscule valves, known as spiracles. Ants do not have blood vessels, but a thin, punctured tube, known as the dorsal aorta, travels along the top of the insect, acting as a heart, pumping fluids around the body. Again, the

THE SECRET LIFE OF AN ARABLE FIELD

nervous system is organised as a cord, which is situated along the ant's body, with branches reaching out to the whole system.

The majority of insects have compound eyes, and the ant is no exception. These eyes are formed of many little lenses and they easily detect small movements, although they do not often give a sharp image. Small simple eyes, located on the top of their head, allow the ant to determine the polarisation and levels of light. Their head antennae operate to gauge chemicals, air currents and general vibrations present in an area. The very strong jaws of the ant are used to carry objects, build nests and to resist attack. The abdomen is the place where all the internal organs are found. Worker ants do not have reproductive organs, but instead exhibit stings which they use against prey. It is only the occasional reproductive females, males and queen that have wings.

When the temperature and humidity are right, these winged ants of both sexes emerge and begin their nuptial flight. Female queens mate with various males during this flight, then go to start a new colony, finding a safe place to lay their eggs. The males do not survive this flight, and the females will chew off their own wings for nutrition once they have landed. Some ant colonies will show distinctly different sizes of ants, depending on their role within the group, with soldier ants having bigger jaws to aid them in fighting.

Most ants give birth to a new generation once a year. An ant will be born female with two sets of chromosomes, (one from each parent), if the egg is fertilised. If the egg is not fertilised the resultant ant will be male, with a single set of unpaired chromosomes. The ant develops from the larvae stage to a pupa and then to an adult, showing complete metamorphosis. As larvae, ants are helpless, and the worker ants will nourish them by regurgitating food from what is known as the 'social stomach'. As the larvae develop, more solid food, such as unfertilised eggs, prey and seeds are given.

It takes four to five moults before the larvae reach the pupal stage. The role an ant will play in the community will be affected by the food that it has eaten as larva, although genetics and the environment are thought to influence it too.

All worker ants are wingless females. At the beginning of her life she will look after the queen and larvae. Then she will commence digging, enlarging, and looking after the nest. As she grows older, her role becomes defending the nest and looking for food. This is dangerous work, and only older ants who are towards the end of their life span undertake it. Queens are able to survive for up to 30 years whilst a worker has a life expectancy of one to three years. Males tend to survive for just a few weeks. In hotter areas, ants will be busy throughout the year, but in the cooler regions, they hibernate over winter.

Some ant species prevent a female from mating more than once by blocking up her sexual organs with fluids from the males' glands. The number of queens can vary between colonies, with some having none at all. Drone males can mate with a queen from another colony. To begin with he is assaulted by her workers, but when he releases chemicals that impact the group's behaviour, he is taken to the queen to mate.

These pheromones, as well as sound and touch, are the way in which ants communicate with each other. Smell is absorbed through their mobile antennae, which tells the ant about its orientation and intensity. Ants leave a scent trail for other members of their species when they move across the ground, which is especially useful in foraging, and the route is further strengthened as more and more ants pass along it. If there is an obstacle in the path, the leading ants will find a way around it, and the other ants will follow, leaving their scent, and thereby collectively securing the best route. Some species use the magnetic field of the Earth to find direction. Occasionally, ants can become disorientated by the scent trail, and end up going around in circles, until they eventually die. Ants can jump, glide and make bridges over water or chasms. Others form floating rafts.

If an ant meets harm, they will send off a panic pheromone which is picked up by other ants, near and far, creating an attack response. Some ant species have evolved to use 'propaganda' smells, causing chaos and warfare within other ant colonies. Ants pass food to each other, mouth to mouth, along with pheromones, passing information as they do so. Pheromones from the queen also serve as an indicator as to when a new queen should be sought for the colony. Sounds are emitted by rubbing the mandible with the abdomen, allowing ants to exchange information with their own, and maybe other species.

Ants defend themselves by biting and stinging. The sting of some species, for example the jack jumper ant in Australia, can be fatal. Stings in general can contain formic acid, alkaloids and piperidines (which is a severe irritant to the skin and eyes and may cause toxicity to the kidneys if ingested). Jaws themselves can be a very powerful tool. One ant, the *Odontomachus bauri*, is able to shut its jaws in 130 microseconds or at 233km/h. These fast snapping jaws are an extreme weapon. Some ants use their jaws to commit suicide by rupturing their abdomen, thus releasing a corrosive chemical mix onto their attackers.

Older ants serve their colony by being the ones to secure the nest at the end of the day, and subsequently dying in the exposed environment that they find themselves in. Ants need to remove the dead bodies of fellow ants and clean their nest to prevent infection. 'Undertaker' ants are used for this purpose, although it is not their exclusive role. They can tell who is alive, and who is not, by the chemicals they give off, especially oleic acid. They will then dispose of the body in their waste site. This is vital to the fitness of the colony.

Ants can be fairly aggressive. Some species attack other colonies, stealing eggs and larvae, either to consume or utilise as slaves. For example, the Amazon ant does

not forage for its own food but relies instead on hostage workers to do it for them. Some captured ants seek revenge by injuring just the female pupae, the gender solely responsible for their capture, and leaving the passive males. Scent is all important in recognising kin and workmates. Each colony will have a different smell, even within the same species, and ants not exhibiting that smell will be attacked. Parasitic ants do occur, nesting within a host colony and deriving food from it. They do this by entering before the queen has laid her eggs, as the smell of the colony has yet to be established.

Aphids, which produce honeydew from eating plant sap, are highly regarded by ants, which can get the aphid to secrete the energy rich honeydew by hitting them with their antennae. These ants will protect the aphid from harm and may even take them with them when they are changing location. Ants also protect mealybugs for the same reason.

Ants massage the honeydew-producing gland of caterpillars of the Lycaenidae family, which comprise 30% of all known butterflies. They herd together these creatures, taking them to feeding sites by day, and by night to their nest. The grizzled skipper butterfly, common throughout Europe, communicates with the ant by vibrating its wings. Others use sounds. One caterpillar has evolved to emit a smell which is so similar to that of the ants' larvae that it is taken into the ants' nest, where it subsequently eats all of their larvae.

Symbiosis in the ant world can be shown by the fungus cultivation of some ant species, where the fungus is used to capture insect prey up to 50 times larger than the ant. The fungus, growing on bark, is bored into by the ant, creating tiny holes in which the ant hides. Insects, descending on the fungus, will get their feet caught in the holes, at which point the ant grabs them and pulls them further towards the tree. Other ants join in. If the captured insect is large, the ants will just hold on until it exhausts. However, if it is small, the ants will charge through the holes to kill it.

Ants collect nectar from flowers, but they seldom pollinate. It is thought that the secretory, metapleural glands, unique to ants, destroy the viability of the pollen. Plants can work co-operatively with ants, with structures called extra-floral nectaries that form a platform specifically for ants, which in turn reduces the number of insects that potentially damage the plant. Other species create large cavities providing a nesting site for ants, which then go on to distribute and plant seedlings, adding to their growth with manure. These seedlings start to produce their own nesting cavities, and so they proliferate. It is thought that 9% of all plant species utilise the ant in their dispersal of seeds, many of which have evolved to do so; for example, sometimes the seed contains an outer layer, which is food for the ant.

Fungi species assault certain ants by infecting them. The ants die from this contamination and the fungi rules the roost by growing on their dead bodies and bearing fruit in their perfectly created new microhabitat.

Other bizarre relationships are formed by a nematode or roundworm, which poisons certain ants, making areas of their abdomen turn from black to red. This venom also makes the ants hold their abdomens higher, which reaches the attention of birds, thinking that they are fruit, ready to eat. They will then consume the ant. Their bird droppings will be taken, in turn, by more ants to nourish their young, creating a better environment for the original nematode.

Humans value ants for many reasons. They keep down certain pests and ventilate the soil. Weaver ants have been used since 300ad in China as a biological control, protecting citrus fields from beetles and caterpillars. Army ants are used to repair body tissues after surgery or injury. The wound is held together and the ants released onto it. These ants grip the wound's border in their jaws, securely fastening it. The surgeon will then remove the ant's body, leaving its head in place.

Edward Osborne Wilson, a leading world expert on ants, has estimated that for every human, there are 1 million ants alive on the planet. This means that the total biomass of ants equals the biomass of the human population. He has calculated that there are between one and ten quadrillion ants alive at any given time. This is a valuable food source. In Mexico, ant eggs are eaten as caviar. In Columbia, they toast some of their larger ant species. In parts of India, ants are used as a relish with curry, whilst in Thailand, ant eggs and larvae, along with the grown ants, are added to salad. Ant cordial is served in Australia.

Ants are not welcomed everywhere, however. They cause problems to mankind, ranging from damage to buildings and agricultural crops, eating stockpiles of food and getting into water supplies. Pest control realistically focuses on reduction rather than elimination, and this will depend on the species and location.

THE SECRET LIFE OF AN ARABLE FIELD

Aphid

The aphid, also known as blackfly or greenfly, is a small sap-sucking insect belonging to the Aphidoidea family. There are in the region of 5,000 known species. Females are able to give birth to female nymphs, without any male involvement. In temperate parts of the world, sexual reproduction can also take place in autumn, with the eggs going into diapause throughout winter. This results from shorter day lengths, temperature changes or lack of food.

Food supply depends on species, as does the variety of food sources. About 450 species colonise agricultural crops. They suck sap from the plant and carry viruses, leaving honeydew, which creates a sooty mould. Insecticides are not always proficient, as aphids become tolerant, as well as usually being situated on the bottom of the leaves. Because aphids are so small it is difficult to treat them, and they recover populations very quickly. They are, however, prey for the caterpillar of certain hoverfly, as well as ladybirds, aphid midges and lacewing larvae, crab spiders, parasitic wasps and certain fungi. Biological pest control has its limitations in an outside environment, and is best used in greenhouses. Soap and water washes are successful in the garden.

Although aphids have a global distribution, they are most common in temperate regions. They are thought to have evolved 280 million years ago in the Early Permian period. With the absence of bones, aphid fossils are difficult to find, although the first known specimen comes from the Triassic period, 51 to 252 million years ago. When angiosperms, or flowering plants, developed 140 million years ago, aphids were able to specialise and increase in diversity alongside these plants.

Aphids are soft-bodied insects, coloured green, black, pink or transparent. They possess antennae and compound eyes, using their stylet mouthpieces to suck sap. Most aphids are wingless, although at specific times winged versions are produced, allowing the species to move to different plants. This usually occurs when there is too much ecological success on one plant and it becomes too crowded, or too eaten, to continue. It also is a response to predation or for fleeing viral infections.

About 90% of species feed on one type of plant. The remaining 10% will vary their food source throughout the year. The aphid infects a new plant through its saliva when it tests its nutrition levels. They favour sap from phloem, which is made up of 99% more amino acids and sugars compared to the sap of xylem. Phloem sap also flows freely into their mouths, as it is under pressure. However, there are times when an aphid needs xylem sap, such as when they are less fertile. It uses mechanisms in its body to draw up the sap, which is at negative pressure.

Aphids use different hosts on which to reproduce, and 10% of species will chose woody hosts for winter and herbaceous plants for summer. An example of this is the soybean aphid, *Aphis glycines*, which overwinters on buckthorn. Reproduction throughout the year is asexual, producing only female aphids, Males are produced in the run up to winter, who then fertilise the eggs which will hatch the following spring.

Some aphids are actually born pregnant, allowing for population numbers to increase exponentially. A spring born female cabbage aphid, *Brevicoryne brassicae*, can potentially give birth to billions of aphids in a season, resulting from 41 generations. Aphids generally have a life expectancy of 20 to 40 days. In a greenhouse, asexual reproduction carries on throughout the year.

THE SECRET LIFE OF AN ARABLE FIELD

Some ant species have a mutualistic relationship with aphids, where they actively farm them, enjoying the honeydew that aphids produce from their anus. They even stroke the aphids with their antennae. The aphids respond by emitting smaller drops of honeydew, which have a richer level of amino acids. Ants go as far as collecting the aphid eggs to keep in their nests over winter, bringing the newly born aphids back to their plants by carrying them on their backs.

Aphids are preyed upon by a great number of other insects and birds. Songbirds can consume up to a million aphids in a day. They are also affected by bacteria, fungi and viruses. Fungi spores attach themselves to the aphid, and after a period of three days, the fungi has won, releasing further spores into the environment, with secondary fungi often taking up position. Rainfall and temperature, as well as wind, impacts the number of aphids. They protect themselves by forming a gall on the plant, sheltering inside it, even evolving 'soldiers' to protect this swelling. Aphids will fall to the ground to escape danger. Others live there permanently, feeding on roots.

Plants resist aphid attack by releasing chemicals from their leaves. In some plants it is the young leaves that defend themselves, in others, the older. The green peach aphid can transmit over 110 different plant viruses. The presence of honeydew on a plant causes the spread of fungi.

Ash

The European ash, *Fraxinus excelsior*, belongs to the olive family, Oleaceae. It grows throughout Europe, from Trondheim Fjord in Norway, south to the north of Greece, and east to the Alborz Mountains in Iran. The tree has been naturalised in New Zealand and is also found in parts of Canada and the United States.

The ash is known for its 'helicopter seeds', a winged fruit evolved to be carried by the wind. These fruit, also known as 'ash keys', are around 25 to 45mm long, suspended from the tree in bunches over the winter months. If they are planted whilst still green they will take root immediately. However, if the seeds are left until they become brown they will take 18 months to develop, needing the chill of two winters to germinate.

This deciduous tree commonly grows to 12 to 18 metres although it can be double that. The trunk is usually up to 1m in diameter, with an even, greyish bark on juvenile trees, developing into a deep, vertically broken bark on older specimens. Its leaves, which are 20 to 35cm in length, are pinnately compound in that they have 7 to 13 distinct leaflets, arranged in pairs opposite each other, on either side of the stem.

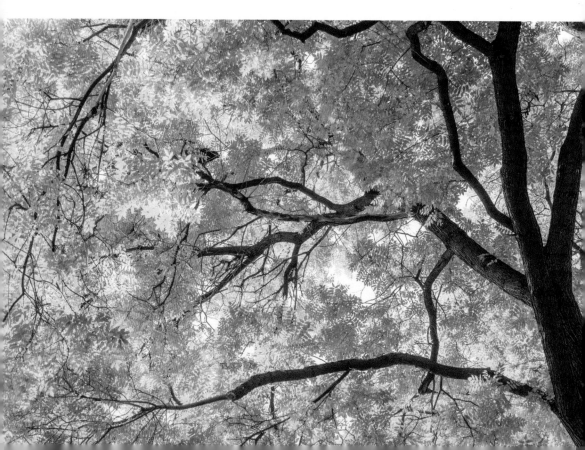

Leaves do not show an autumn colour, and are slow to open in spring and quick to fall in the first frosts of autumn. Usually a tree produces either male or female flowers, but they can change gender from one year to the next, or even exhibit both.

The European ash has black buds, which differentiate it from other ash species, which have grey or brown buds. The mountain ash or rowan, *Sorbus aucuparia*, has alternate leaves with paired stipules, which the European ash lacks.

European ash grows best on moist soils, particularly those with calcareous substrates (those which contain or are formed from calcium carbonate or calcite). Although it does not like the colder regions of Europe it is a pioneer, early succession species, growing preferentially to oak and beech, which are climax or late succession species. The ash does not usually live beyond 250 years of age.

The Biological Records Centre in the UK lists 29 species of insect and mite that feed solely on ash, out of the 111 species that feed on the tree in total. An example of a moth that feeds exclusively on ash is the centre-barred sallow, *Atethmia centrago*. Its larvae will feed on the buds and when it gets older, the flowers and leaves. *Gracillaria syringella* is another moth that feeds on ash, privet and lilac. It causes the darkening of the ash leaves by feeding from within the leaf.

The ash faced real danger in the late 1980s to early '90s, due to the accidental introduction of the emerald ash borer to North America from east Asia. It came over in wooden packing apparatus and rapidly killed tens of millions of ash trees across the USA and Canada. Biological controls, such as three species of Asian wasp, are being investigated.

Ash dieback is due to the fungus, *Hymenoscyphus fraxineus*, which has been particularly prevalent in Europe from the mid-1990s. By 2016 there were warnings that the tree could face extinction in the European continent.

Coppiced ash was used up until the early twentieth century as a sustainable fuel, and as timber for building and woodworking. Ash is a tough, flexible wood, finding uses in bows, tool handles, tennis rackets, skis, oars, walking and hockey sticks. Early aircraft design made use of these qualities too. The wood is almost pure white, although its darker heartwood has a low resistance to ground contact, decaying in five years or so. It is therefore not used for fencing posts. Ash is widely used in making contemporary furniture, doors, veneers and wood flooring.

The Norse people of Scandinavia worshipped the ash as a sacred tree. They believed Odin, the leader of the gods, created the first man out of an ash tree. Legend has it that Yggdrasil, the Tree of the World, had roots that stretched to hell, and branches that reached to heaven, with its trunk joining the two.

Badger

The badger, *Meles meles*, also known as the European badger, is native to most parts of Europe and also western Asia. It is a member of the Mustelidae family, along with several other badger species. In 2012, there were an estimated 300,000 badgers in the UK, with 45,000 killed annually on the roads. They are found in deciduous and mixed woodlands, pastures and scrub. They can live at an altitude of up to 2,000m.

The badger is a powerful, muscular animal, with a small head covered in black, brown, grey and white fur, with a short tail and tiny black eyes. They have five toes to each foot, with strong, non-retractable claws to dig. These claws wear away as the badger ages, with some older badgers losing them almost entirely. Snouts are also utilised for burrowing, and are strong and flexible. Whiskers decorate their snouts and over the eyes. Boars are bigger than sows, but sows have fluffier tails. European badgers are not able to flex their backs as can other members of the Mustelidae family, nor can they stand upright, but they can cover a lot of ground quickly at a gallop. An adult will typically be 25 to 30cm in height at the shoulder and 60 to 90cm in body length, with a 12 to 14cm tail.

The badger hibernates over the winter. It reaches a weight of 15 to 17kg in autumn, utilising its fat reserves in its winter sleep such that it is 7 to 13kg when it emerges in spring. If it is a mild winter in the UK, they may not have a prolonged sleep, emerging above ground during warmer periods. As badgers do not react to red light it is thought that they see in black and white, reacting only to movement.

Two distinctive black bands pass from the upper lip to behind the ears, fusing with the upper body. Similarly, a white band starts at the tip of the nose, going through the forehead and crown. White markings occur on the lower head and travel back towards the neck. Melanistic, erythristic and albino (blacker, redder, or whiter) badgers have been recorded.

The badger is both crepuscular and nocturnal, spending the day sleeping in the vast network of burrows that can be 1.6 to 3.3km long. These chambers encompass many setts, and are home to several families, or clans, of badgers, with a number of entrances. Some of these setts have been used for generations of badgers. Badgers are fastidious about cleanliness, changing the bedding and getting rid of waste. They have toilet areas in specially chosen areas of their territory. Nesting chambers are about 75 x 75 x 38cm, with burrows typically being 22 to 63cm wide

THE SECRET LIFE OF AN ARABLE FIELD

and 14 to 32cm high. The nest will be at least a metre underground, at about 5 to 10m from the entrance.

In the UK, badgers can share their setts with foxes and even rabbits. They offer protection to the rabbit, who takes precautions against the badger by burrowing into smaller, distant cavities. The racoon dog (*Nyctereutes procyonoides*), native to east Asia but now found in many parts of Europe, can over-winter in the same burrows. This works as the badger hibernates two weeks earlier than the racoon dog, and finishes two weeks later. The badger is known to kill the racoon dog if it does not behave.

The badger is a carnivore, feasting on earthworms, bigger insects (e.g. caterpillars, leatherjackets, wasp and bumblebee nests, chafers, ground and dung beetles), smaller mammals (such as rabbits, mice, hedgehogs, moles and shrews) and carrion. Other delicacies include large birds, small reptiles and amphibians. They are impervious to bee stings, even in swarms, as their thick fur protects them from harm. They also enjoy plant food, such as cereals, windfall apples, blackberries, acorns, plums, pears, raspberries, beech mast, fungi, pignuts and root tubers. They will eat clover and grass when other food is unavailable. They usually eat their food *in situ* rather than taking it to their sett. Although it is rare, they are known to kill chickens, killing more than they can eat. They will prey on young rabbits, smelling them out, and digging down to get them. Adult rabbits are not usually taken, unless they are already wounded. They will eat the animal by turning them inside out, and devouring the meat, leaving the skin and fur. They do the same with hedgehogs. It is thought that badgers can kill lambs, as wool and bones have been found in the vicinity of setts, although it could have been a fox who might have shared the sett, as badgers are not known to take food to their chamber.

A sow will give birth to up to five cubs in the spring. She is fertile throughout the year. A boar can mate from 12 to 15 months. A boar will remain with a sow for life, but she will have more than one partner. The gestation period is seven weeks, with cubs generally making their appearance from mid-January to mid-March. If the soil is waterlogged the cubs will be born above ground. The dominant sow may kill the cubs of subordinate sows. Over half of the cubs may be sired by boars from different colonies.

To begin with cubs are pink with silvery fur. Their eyelids are not yet open. They venture out into the open air at 8 weeks, and are weaned at 12 weeks, although they continue to suckle until 4 to 5 months. They gain their adult coat at 6 to 9 weeks and will generally stay with the natal group. A badger can live for 15 years.

Badger setts are used for generations. There can be as many as 50 entrances to a sett and they can house a large number of families, each using their own thoroughfares. Bedding, made up of grass, bracken, straw, moss and leaves is collected during a dry spell, with up to 30 collections in a single night. Badgers are very particular about cleanliness. They undergo an extensive cleaning spell in early spring to prepare for the birth of the cubs, and engage in changing the bedding frequently over the summer to stop the spread of parasites.

In the case of a badger death, the rest of the clan either seal off the body within a chamber or take it outside to bury.

Clans are generally made up of six badgers, although groups of 23 have been known. Clan size is related to food and habitat conditions. Where food is plentiful, badger ranges can be 30ha, but this increases to 150ha in not so beneficial areas. Boundaries are marked by toilet areas and well-travelled paths, and it is usually the boars that are responsible for guarding their territory. There is a dominant and submissive structure in both boars and sows. Larger boars venture into another territory during the spring mating season. This is when most of the fights occur. They will bite their opponent on the neck and rump, and chase them down, sometimes with fatal results. A badger will growl if under attack and make deep 'kekkering' noises when fighting.

THE SECRET LIFE OF AN ARABLE FIELD

They have a wide range of vocalisations, including barking in shock, whickering when playing or upset, and screaming if disturbed.

Badgers can be deadly when provoked. Due to their innate aggression when cornered they have few predators. Across Europe they face danger from the grey wolf (*Canis lupus*), the Eurasian lynx (*Lynx lynx*) and brown bears (*Ursus arctos*), although these carnivores usually prefer easier prey such as deer. In the UK, it is the large domestic dog which causes problems to the badger. Other predators include the golden eagle (*Aquila chrysaetos*), which attacks both cubs and weak adults.

Badgers suffer from bovine tuberculosis (bovine TB). Although this can kill the badger, they can live for years whilst infected. The disease was first documented in Switzerland in 1951 where badgers were believed to have caught it from chamois (*Rupicapra rupicapra*) or roe deer (*Capreolus capreolus*). Twenty years later, in 1971, it showed up in the UK in cows. The southwest of England, Wales and Ireland have been particularly affected. There is huge disagreement over whether culling the badger population will help stem the disease. Culling has taken place in regions where TB has been prevalent, but a subsequent reduction in TB in cattle has yet to be proved.

Gassing was the preferred form of culling in the UK until the 1980s, when vaccination became an option. Vets were generally in favour of culling, rather than an injection, as they said that bovine TB causes a lot of suffering in the badger population. A limited cull was granted by the Department for Environment, Food and Rural Affairs (Defra) in 2012, but this was postponed for various reasons until August 2013. Some 5,000 badgers were then killed in a six-week period in the west of Somerset and Gloucester, using both controlled shooting (where badgers were trapped in cages) and free shooting by marksmen. However, the cost of the operation was said to be more expensive than any savings made. There is still ambiguity over the best course of action.

Badgers also suffer from mustelid herpesvirus-1, rabies and canine distemper, although only the former is present in the UK. A large number of badgers were culled in Europe in the 1960s and 1970s to curb rabies.

Badgers are killed by several methods. They can be smoked out of their sett, caught in jaw traps, shot, or dug out by specifically bred dogs such as the fox terrier or dachshund. However, shotgun pellets do not do any damage to their incredibly thick skulls and skin, and long hair acts to defend them in many circumstances.

The sport of badger baiting used to be extremely popular, but is now banned. Badgers would be caught and caged, whereupon they would be set upon by dogs. The Cruelty to Animals Act of 1835, followed by the Protection of Animals Act of 1911 outlawed this practice in the UK. The 1992 Protection of Badgers Act makes cruelty and death of a badger a criminal offence, as well as protecting the badger from sett disruption, or capture. The penalty is six months in prison, a fine of up to £5,000, community service and/or a ban from dog-ownership. Capture to help a distressed or injured badger is exempt.

The hams from badgers used to be smoked and eaten in the UK. Many parts of the badger can be utilised for oils and ointments. Their hair has been used for hundreds of years to make sporrans for Scottish Highlanders. The pouch is created from the pelt, with a badger's head forming the flap. The pelt also used to be used for pistol furniture. Badger hair has very high water-retention properties, which makes it invaluable for making shaving brushes. These days, the majority of badger hair is exported from China, where they have special farms. They produce three grades of hair, used to make the brushes.

The name badger probably dates back to the sixteenth century, coming from the word badge, delineating the white mark on their forehead. Another source could be the French word for digger – 'bêcheur'. Pre-dating this is the Old English word 'brocc' or Scottish 'brock', which comes from the Celtic word meaning grey. Other names were used up until the eighteenth century, such as 'bawson' meaning striped in white; 'pate' in use in the north of England; 'earth dog' in the south of Ireland; and 'mochyn daear' or earth pig, in use in Wales.

The species can be traced back to the early Pleistocene, up to 1.8 million years ago. The modern animal evolved in the early Middle Pleistocene, 781,000 to 126,000 years ago, although badger remains have been found pre-dating this. Evolutionary changes in their teeth show the badger has become increasingly omnivorous, since the molar surface area has enlarged over time. They have a very powerful bite, and can crush bones, including those of humans.

Bank Vole

The bank vole, *Myodes glareolus*, is the UK's smallest vole, smaller than the field vole, water vole and Orkney vole. It is found across Europe, western Siberia and northwest Asia. It was accidentally but successfully introduced to Ireland in the 1950s, although there are concerns that it is supplanting the native wood mouse. It is absent from most of the Channel Islands and Scottish islands, as well as the Isles of Scilly. There is a subspecies on the island of Skomer in west Wales, which is a much bigger vole, known as the Skomer vole. The bank vole is found in grassland, heath and moorland, farmland, field verges, woods and in towns and gardens, enjoying dense vegetation, for example bracken and bramble.

It measures 8 to 12cm long, with an additional 4 to 6cm tail. It is a rich, chestnut brown colour, with a white underbelly. Weighing between 15 to 40g, it has a lifespan of one to two years, although this increases to nearly four years in captivity. Voles are known to have rounder faces than mice, with smaller ears, eyes and tails. As they do not hibernate, they can be seen throughout the year.

The bank vole is on the go both night and day. It listens to bird calls, which warn it of danger. It consumes fruits, nuts and small insects, especially enjoying hazelnuts and blackberries. Bank voles feed on buds, bark and leaves as well, climbing several metres into hedgerows and trees, such as beech, larch and maple. They are considered to be a pest as they eat the new shoots of developing trees, thereby diminishing the natural regrowth of woodland. However, predators, such as the red fox, least weasel, stoat, kestrel and tawny owl all help keep numbers down. Voles protect themselves by burrowing or using habitual paths. They are not shy, and will make their way to a bird table, although their shorter tail, in relation to their body, makes them less agile than a mouse. They dig branching burrows with many entrances, lined with moss, feathers and plant fibres, but will nest above ground in round, grass structures if the soil is inappropriate.

Each female has a home range of approximately 500 to 2,000m². Males have a much bigger home range, and this includes several female territories within it. Breeding takes place between May to September, with a gestation period of three weeks or a bit longer if the female is weaning previous pups. Males can kill existing pups before mating with their mother, and a female can kill another female's young. The female gives birth to three to four litters each summer, with three to five pups in each litter. These take just over three weeks to wean, with the female pups becoming sexually mature at six weeks. The male pups can reproduce in eight weeks. There is a population boom in the summer months.

Bank voles often carry the Puumala virus, which can cause a haemorrhagic fever in humans, and in 0.5% of cases, lead to death. This virus has evolved with the bank vole. It does not affect the vole, although it does appear to increase winter mortality. The bank vole is susceptible to poisoning from car fumes, as well as pesticides and rodenticides.

Barley

Barley, (*Hordeum vulgare*), is a self-pollinating member of the grass family. It was one of the first cultivated grains and remains an important cereal crop in the temperate regions of the world today. Some 149 million tons of barley were grown in the world in 2017, with the four most important producers being: Russia with 20.6 million tons, Australia 13.5 million tons, Germany 10.9 million tons and France with 10.5 million tons. The UK was not far behind, with 7.2 million tons.

Barley is the fourth most popular grain, after maize, rice and wheat. The USA uses half of their barley to create livestock feed. Barley is also used to make beer, whisky and malt, and is widely employed in health foods. Barley can cope with greater salinity in the soil compared to wheat, which suggests why it is so popular in the early days of its cultivation. It was first domesticated in the Fertile Crescent, an area to the west of Asia, and alongside the productive grounds of the Nile in northeast Africa. It was developed at the same time as the ancient einkorn wheat and its derivative emmer wheat, at around 10,000bc, and was spreading across Eurasia by 2,000bc.

It is thought that beer making goes right back to Neolithic times, when barley was first cultivated. Barley was valuable enough to be considered a good source of currency. The Ancient Egyptians feature barley in their hieroglyphs. The goddess Shala in early Mesopotamia, located between the Euphrates and Tigris rivers, is represented by a stem of barley. A clay tablet, dating back to 2,350bc, from the time of King Urukagina in Iraq, has shown the rationing of barley, with 30 to 40 pints allowed monthly for adults, and 20 pints each for children. In Ancient Rome, gladiators were known as *hordearii*, or 'barley eaters'. Historians believe that Eurasian societies have remained dominant as a result of their farming activities and foodstuff, including barley. Whilst historically, barley was cheap enough to be available to everyone, potatoes made a surge in popularity in the nineteenth century.

Wild barley, the precursor to the crop, can be found from Crete to Tibet. It has a productive central spike, with the other two spikes not so efficient. Domesticated barley either has two spikes, where it is known as two-row barley, or six spikes (arranged in six rows around the stalk), where it is known as six-row barley. Two-row barley has a higher fermentable sugar content. Six-row barley, with a higher protein

content, is predominantly used for animal feed. The lower protein levels in two-row barley make beer less cloudy. Britain and Germany both favour this for beer, whilst the United States prefers six-row barley. Ireland and Scotland predominantly use green beer – which has only gone through primary distillation – to distil whisky. Barley wine was made in England in the eighteenth century, by boiling the barley in water and adding white wine, borage, lemon and sugar. During the Second World War, the Italians used barley instead of coffee.

Hulless barley, also termed 'naked' barley, has been cultivated for centuries. The tough, inedible, outer hull is only loosely attached to the kernel. This is especially useful for animal feed, as the grain is easier to digest. Pearl barley has been steamed and processed to withdraw the outer hull and some of the bran. It cooks more quickly than hulled barley and is the most common form of barley for human use.

THE SECRET LIFE OF AN ARABLE FIELD

100g of raw barley contains 20% or more of the Daily Value of protein, B vitamins, niacin, manganese, phosphorous and other essential nutrients and minerals. It is made up of 77% carbohydrates, only 1% fat, 10% protein and 10% water. It is thought to lower cholesterol and regulate glucose production. Like wheat and rye, barley contains gluten, although some individuals with a wheat allergy can tolerate barley.

A great many cultivars have been developed. Some of the British ones are 'Maris Otter', an English two-row winter crop, derived from the parent cultivars 'Proctor' and 'Pioneer' and used to produce malt for British beers. 'Bere' is a six-row variety, grown in the Orkney Islands, for use in beer production. 'Golden Promise' is a semi-dwarf Scottish variety, utilised in beer and whisky production.

The word 'barn' comes from the Old English words *bærlic-croft*, meaning 'barley house', first recorded in around 966ad. *Hordeum*, the Latin genus name, comes from the Indo-European word for 'bristly', referring to the spikes on the ears of barley.

England had an unusual use for barley. Barleycorns were used for measurement, with three to four barleycorns making an inch, and four to five poppy seeds to every barleycorn. Until the nineteenth century, an inch was three barleycorns, although this was later superseded by standardisation. However, a barleycorn is still defined as 'a former unit of measurement (about a third of an inch) based on the length of a grain of barley.' To this day, shoe sizes in both the UK and USA still use the barleycorn measurement, although modern varieties of barleycorn now vary in length.

Barn Owl

The barn owl, *Tyto alba*, belongs to the *Tytonidae* family. They are extremely widespread, being found practically everywhere in the world, with the exception of desert and polar areas, Indonesia and some of the Pacific islands, and regions just north of the Himalayan mountains. Barn owls are typically found in open country, such as farmland, grassland or sparsely wooded areas. They usually live in areas below 2,000m above sea level, but can be found as high as 3,000m.

There are about 28 subspecies of the barn owl. They measure 33 to 39cm long, with a wingspan of 80 to 95cm and weight of 250 to 350g. There are thought to be 4,000 breeding pairs in the UK, with an estimated 110,000 to 220,000 pairs living in Europe. They have a white, heart shaped face, buff brown head, back and wings, and white underparts. Although found across the whole of the UK, serious declines have occurred, especially in the 1950s and 1960s, due to organochlorine pesticides.

Barn owls usually become active just before dusk. They have exceptionally good hearing, and identify their prey using sound. They do not hunt by sight. Their diet consists mainly of mice, voles, shrews, rats and smaller birds. These owls seem impartial to earthworms, even when there is a scarcity of other food. Across the world they also consume lizards, bats, insects and amphibians.

Barn owl ears are not symmetrical – one ear is set higher; allowing them to work out the position and distance of prey more effectively. Barn owls make no noise when they fly, due to the tiny saw-like edges to their flight feathers, which minimise turbulence. They fly slowly, hovering where they think there might be terrestrial prey. Each owl eats one to three voles or a comparable mass every day, which is 23% of the bird's weight. Excess food is stored at the roosts. With small prey, bones and fur will all be digested; however, with larger food, such as rabbits and rats, indigestible parts of the prey are thrown away.

Barn owls are not particularly territorial. However, they do have a home range from which to feed. This is about 1km from their nest, making an area of approximately 300 hectares. Breeding pairs hunt in the same range, but out of the breeding season they will roost in different sites, which are smaller than the nest area.

Barn owls pair for life, although if their mate is killed, they will form a new partnership. They can breed from 10 to 11 months old. The breeding season is long, starting in February or March, with the birds capable of having two broods each year if there are sufficient prey populations. The female lays four to seven chalky white eggs

in a nest constructed in a tree hollow, disused building or cliff. In the UK buildings are preferred as they are more sheltered from the rain. She will incubate these eggs for 32 to 34 days, whilst her mate provides her with food. Hatching success with a good food supply is in the region of 75%. The new chicks are born with a white downy coat, which is replaced with creamy down after 12 days. Like other birds of prey, she regurgitates her pellets, comprising the indigestible parts of her diet, including plant matter, fur and feathers. This keeps the chicks insulated. They fledge at 8 to 10 weeks of age, when she will teach them how to hunt.

The barn owl does not actually hoot. Instead it vocalises a long shriek. Courting males utter a sharp twitter, whilst they hiss like a snake when disturbed. They have different calls for pleasure and defence. If captured the barn owl will fling itself on its back and protect itself with its sharp talons.

Barn owls are hunted in the UK by the golden eagle, northern goshawk and the common buzzard. As these raptors are protected, their numbers are growing to the

detriment of the barn owl. In the wild, barn owls can expect to live to four years of age; however, there is a high mortality rate of 66 to 75% each year, with only 33% getting through their first year. In captivity, barn owls have lived to 25 years. In temperate regions, most will die of starvation, especially young getting through their first winter. Road deaths and powerlines are another threat, and shooting, particularly in the Mediterranean region, is a problem. Pesticide use continues to be a menace.

In Britain, barn owls are sedentary. Young will settle about 9km from their birthplace, usually along river corridors. In other areas of the world they can travel a lot further. Apart from the peregrine falcon, the barn owl is thought to be most widely distributed of all birds, with the IUCN estimating nearly 10 million individuals. Agricultural intensification, leading to the loss of grassland habitats and nesting sites, has affected the barn owl, as has the use of pesticides and rodenticides, especially in European and North American populations. They are therefore considered a subject of concern in these regions.

Nest boxes are a way of increasing populations, whilst also giving scientists a chance to observe the bird. The owls are a good substitution for rodenticides, as the resident owls will keep down the population of rats, making it a popular switch for farmers.

Historically, these birds have been feared and given the name 'death owl' and 'ghost owl', with the incorrect belief that they prey on chickens and cats.

Beech

F*agus sylvatica* is the European beech. Other genus are present in the family Fagaceae; deciduous trees that are found in temperate regions across Asia, Europe and North America. However, the beech is not considered native to Britain. It is thought that Stone Age man brought it over when the English Channel was created some 450,000 years ago. It is found extensively in the south of England and is still considered as non-native in the north, where it is removed from 'native' woods.

However, the beech hedge in the village of Meikleour, near Perth is said to be over 250 years old. Legend has it that it was being planted in 1745, when Bonnie Prince Charlie landed, and the men dropped their tools and took up arms. They were away for over a year, by which time the hedge had taken off. It was subsequently allowed to grow as a reminder of the battles. It now stands 33m high and is 550m long.

Beech trees can grow to 50 metres, exhibiting a 3 metre diameter, although they are more commonly 30 metres tall. A 10-year-old sapling stands at 4 metres, and the tree will live to see 150 to 200, if not 300, years. They are harvested usually between 80 to 100 years. If it grows in a woodland setting, a beech will grow taller, with higher branches that are trying to see the light; however, in an open setting, the tree will be shorter with more extensive branching.

The trees are marcescent, whereby they retain their leaves over winter and undergo abscission (dropping the leaves) in the spring, making them an attractive hedge. They need a humid atmosphere, with plenty of rain throughout the year, and do best on a well-drained soil. Their roots do not like to sit in a lot of stagnant water, so clay is not the best option. However, they can grow well in different soil types, particularly enjoying calcified or slightly acidic earth. The tree can be found at altitudes of 600m above sea level.

Beeches dominate oaks and elm in the south of the UK, from the south of Norfolk to Cardigan in Wales. North of this, oaks will take over. Beech trees do not like direct sunlight; indeed, beech forests are very dark places. Bluebells are characteristically found in beech woods, enjoying the chemical composition of the soil from the leaf litter.

10% of forests in France are made up of beech. Ukraine and Romania are home to huge virgin forests of this tree; their climax communities containing the largest predators in Europe – the brown bear, the lynx and the grey wolf. These forests are up to 500 years old and cover thousands of acres of untouched ecology.

Buds develop in response to day length and temperature. Summer temperatures and rainfall determine how many leaves grow the following year. Terminal buds can excrete hormones that stall the development of extra buds. Each bud can grow into a shoot containing at least ten leaves.

Beech cultivars have been developed since the beginning of the nineteenth century, including the copper beech, *Fagus sylvatica purpurea*, with deep purple leaves, and many, such as Dawyck Purple, (named after Dawyck Botanic Garden in the Scottish Borders), have gone on to achieve the Royal Horticultural Society's Award of Garden Merit.

Beech is widely used as firewood. It splits well under the axe and burns for hours with a tranquil flame. It is used in beer-making to line the bottom of the fermentation tank, on which the yeast settles. It does not clog up, as this would contaminate the flavour of the drink. It is also used to smoke certain sausages and cheeses.

Beech can be used as an alternative to maple and birch to make drums, giving a tone somewhere between the two. The fabric modal, a type of rayon, is created from reconstituted cellulose from beech wood pulp, and is superior to that from other broadleaved trees. The wood is used for furniture framing, flooring and engineering. It can also be used in rifle manufacture instead of walnut. With its short and fine

THE SECRET LIFE OF AN ARABLE FIELD

grain, it is easily handled, soaked, dyed and glued, aided by steaming the wood. It has a density of 720kg per cubic meter, but it is not suitable for heavy, structural work.

Beech nuts or mast are contained within the small burrs that fall in autumn. These little nuts are triangular, and are edible for humans and animals, although not in great amounts as they contain tannins and alkaloids. They hold enough oil to be used for cooking and were used in lamps in the nineteenth century. The nuts can also be ground, creating flour from which the tannins can be removed by soaking. Young leaves are added to gin, straining it off after a few weeks to give a spirit called beech leaf noyau. Spring leaves taste like cabbage and can be used in salads.

The Indo-Europeans, prehistoric people of Eurasia, who we learn of primarily from linguistic reconstruction and some archaeology, lived at the end of the Neolithic Age, around 2,000bc. They are said to have used beech bark to write on, particularly in religious work. Subsequent Europeans cultures have copied their example. As a result, the word for book in many languages is extremely similar to the word for beech. For example, in modern German, book is 'buch', whilst beech tree is 'buche'. In Sweden, 'bok' means both book and beech tree. In Old English, 'bōc', and the Old Norse, 'bók' both mean beech tree as well as referring to a book. The English word 'book' is derived from the Old English 'bōk'.

Silver and Downy Birch

Silver birch, *Betula pendula*, and downy birch, *Betula pubescens*, are deciduous trees belonging to the Betulaceae family. Silver birch prefers dry, acid, sandy soils and is found throughout Europe and southwest Asia, ranging from Siberia and China to the mountainous regions of Turkey and into north Iran. Downy birch, by contrast, enjoys the wet clay soils and peat bogs of northern Europe and north Asia. Downy birch is renowned for inhabiting regions further north than all other broadleaf trees, with the variety *B.p. var. pumila* being native to both Iceland and Greenland, historically covering Iceland in rich woodland.

Silver birch grows 15 to 25m, sometimes more. It is named after its silver trunk, which exhibits a white, flaking bark and is usually around 40cm in diameter. This bark starts off a smooth, golden-brown colour and as the tree ages it thickens and becomes pale and papery, in a manner akin to the paper birch, *B. papyrifera*. Silver birch is differentiated from downy birch in that it has hairless, warty shoots, whereas downy birch has hairy shoots without the warts. The downy birch is a slightly smaller tree, standing 10 to 20m high, with a thicker diameter of 70cm. Silver birch, by nature, has a paler bark with fewer, black fissures, and shows more triangulation in its leaves than downy birch. The leaves of silver birch are coarsely double-toothed, whilst downy birch has finely serrated leaf margins. Silver birch also requires more warmth than downy birch, and is therefore found in temperate regions of Australia and the US, to which it has been introduced. Both trees form wind-pollinated catkins in the early spring. Seeds are 1 to 2mm long, and are winged at both sides. They ripen towards the end of the summer.

Both these birches are pioneer species. Silver birch will regenerate wasteland or an area after a forest fire. It is specifically used in polluted areas, growing extensively in cities and industrial areas, although its ease of pollination has meant it is considered invasive in certain US states and Canada. Downy birch is also a pioneer species, but is eventually replaced by taller trees, causing the demise of the birch as the shade created by the other trees prevent further birch seedlings from growing.

The open canopy of these trees creates a massive diversity of mosses and grasses below, which provide a fertile ground for insect life. The light that hits the ground through the open crowns of the trees allows plants such as violets, primroses, bluebells, wood anemones and wood sorrel to grow. Bilberry and cowberry also benefit.

THE SECRET LIFE OF AN ARABLE FIELD

Silver Birch

Birds, such as the green woodpecker, nightingale, tree pipit, chaffinches and willow warbler all find their home within a birch wood.

The fungus *Taphrina betulina* creates the 'witch's broom' effect in the tangled twigs of silver birch. This tree benefits from the mycorrhizal relationship with the mushroom *Amanita muscaria*, allowing it to grow in acidic or sandy soils, which are low in nutrients. Birches support over 500 species of insect, including 106 beetles and 105 butterflies and moths, with 133 insects feeding exclusively on them. Researchers in Greenland have identified over 70 species of fungi growing on downy birch.

The disease birch dieback is more prevalent on planted trees, with naturally grown trees seemingly less affected.

Silver birch is a pale wood, with no noticeable heartwood. It is useful for furniture, veneers, parquet flooring, coffins, skis, woodworking, and as firewood. In years gone by, its bark was utilised in tanning leather, as the bark contains high levels of tannin, which also allows it to be used as a preservative. Resin gained from heating the bark can be used as waterproof glue. Silver birch is good for starting fires, whilst the twigs are useful for kindling wood. Bark can be ground up and made into bark bread, which was a popular choice in times of famine, with the inner bark being mixed with wheat flour. The bark can be taken from the tree without causing any harm to it, and this was once such a common practice that Carl Linnaeus, the eighteenth century Swedish botanist, became alarmed. Racing jumps are commonly made from birch wood as are brooms.

Birch trees can be tapped, giving a sugary liquid similar to maple syrup. This can be further fermented to give wine or ale. It is done in spring, when the sap begins to rise up the trunk, bringing sugars from the roots to the deciduous trees' twigs, supplying the energy needed to grow new shoots and leaves. In parts of the former USSR this is done on a commercial scale, creating cosmetics such as shampoos and medicines, as well as food.

The outside of the bark is rich in botulin (20%). Essential oil is made from the buds. Triterpene levels in the bark are found to have anti-inflammatory, anti-cancer and anti-viral qualities. Oil, derived from the bark, is a good insect repellent.

Bramble

The bramble, *Rubus fruticosus*, is virulent across the British Isles. It is a member of the rose family, Rosaceae. It cannot be contained by pruning as it emits arching branches with suckering roots that propagate the shrub. It is extremely hardy, growing rapidly in woodland, scrub, hedgerows and ditches, tolerating the poor soils of wasteland. Blackberries, the fruit, can be picked from late summer to early autumn and are an essential favourite in blackberry and apple pie.

The word 'bramble' itself means an unpassable thicket. Bramble is defined as prickly shrubs of the genus *Rubus*, which include raspberries, blackberries and also roses. Traditionally however, in Britain the bramble refers to the blackberry plant. Over 375 species of blackberry are documented, with a range across Europe, temperate areas of Asia, the Americas, and northwest Africa.

Flowers or fruit are not present on the plant until the second year of its growth. Blooms appear in late spring/early summer and are 2 to 3cm wide with five white/pale pink petals. Blackberries are made up of about 20 stand-alone ovaries developed in a single flower. These individual units are called drupelets, and form the aggregate fruit. Drupelets are dependent on pollinators to grow, and bad weather conditions, such as rain or too hot a day will cause reduced activity in the pollinators. Other causes of poor drupelet development are pollen borne viruses, or a lack of nutrients in the roots.

Brambles are important in the eco-system. Many butterflies enjoy the nectar present in their flowers, as do hoverflies, such as *Volucella pellucens*. Butterfly and moth larvae relish the leaves, birds and mammals eat the fruit. Deer also savour the leaves. Seeds are dispersed by birds and small mammals, as well as by larger ones such as the fox and badger.

Phasmatodea, or stick insects, also eat the leaves. However, young leaves can be toxic to many species, and it takes up until their third instar – or two moults – for the insect to build up a resistance. Bramble leaves are the staple diet for stick insects in captivity.

The plant is good to burn, in that its stem contains many tiny airholes, as well as sediments of oil. Bramble can be used as shelter for game birds, for protection of property and for reducing the instance of wild animals thieving from crops and taking livestock. Different species are grown ornamentally for their flowers, e.g. *R. trilobus*; for stems, *R. cockburnianus*; and for ground cover, *R. tricolor*.

The bramble, once established, is very difficult to get rid of as any roots remaining in the soil will redevelop. Obviously, in areas of massive growth and where other plants

are present, it would damage the eco-system too much to dig up all the roots. In this case, chemical control is the only method available. The brambles should first be cut to ground level in the spring and emerging shoots can be sprayed. Chemicals should be chosen with care. There are some on the market that will affect only synthesising dicots or dicotyledons, i.e. those with two embryonic leaves or cotyledons, such as the bramble. Grass and other monocotyledons, such as the daffodil and bluebell, are left unharmed.

The Haraldskær Woman, who lived around 2,500 years ago in what is now Denmark, was found preserved in a peat bog in 1835. She was found to have blackberries in her stomach. Blackberries have been documented in cooking for some time: in jam-making, desserts, pies and jellies. Indeed, in 1696 the *London Pharmacopoeia* refers to the use of blackberries in making wines and cordials. A letter from 1771 advocates the use of the entire plant to treat stomach ulcers. Native Americans and the Ancient

THE SECRET LIFE OF AN ARABLE FIELD

Greeks shared something in common as they used parts of the plant to treat various complaints, among them: leaf shoots to create a tea for bleeding gums and mouth infections; leaf, bark and roots for whooping cough; roots for the intestine – their astringent properties helping diarrhoea; and scurvy, treated by the high vitamin C content of the fruit.

As well as vitamin C, blackberries contain a high percentage of vitamins K and dietary fibre, as well as decent amounts of folic acid and manganese. Their seeds are rich in omega-3 and omega-6, and are good sources of protein, carotenoids, ellagitannins, and the antioxidant ellagic acid. It is the anthocyanins in the blackberry which give it its colour.

Numerous cultivars have been created. James Harvey Logan developed the loganberry in 1880 in the US, which was a blackberry-raspberry hybrid. This was further bred in 1921 to be thornless, but as a result, flavour was lost. The plant hybridises easily, with thornless cultivars developed in the last 30 years in the US, allowing for more effective machine harvesting, better quality fruit and flavour, and higher yields. Mexico is the market leader of blackberry production today, widely using the 'Tupy' cultivar until 2018. They produced enough to feed the whole of Europe and North America when they were out of season. In 2017, the US state of Oregon managed to produce 19,000 imperial tons of blackberries on 6,300 acres ($25km^2$). The John Innes Centre in Norwich developed a semi-erect, thornless cultivar, which was taken on by researchers in the US to create further hybrids.

Blackberries and raspberries fall in the same genus and can suffer similar pests diseases, as well as related cures. Anthracnose is a disease that creates an unbalanced ripening and reduced sap flow. The spotted-wing drosophila, *Drosophila suzukii*, enjoys rotten fruit and will lay its eggs under the blackberry's skin. The blackberry aphid, *Amphorophora rubi*, consumes both blackberry and raspberry fruit. There is also a raspberry beetle, a raspberry moth and a strawberry blossom weevil, which all eat the blackberry. The raspberry bushy dwarf virus creates an infection.

In the UK, moulds such as *Botryotinia* affect the fruit in wet weather, causing them to become toxic. The old wives' tale that fruit of the bramble should not be picked after Old Michaelmas Day on 10 October, since the devil has ruined them, may well ring true for this reason. Christ's crown of thorns is believed by some to have been constructed from brambles, although the hawthorn (*Crataegus*) or crown of thorns plant (*Euphorbia milii*) may have been used instead.

Brimstone Butterfly

It is thought that the word 'butterfly' comes from this species, *Gonepteryx rhamni*, due to the pale-yellow colouration of its wings, i.e. butter-coloured fly. Brimstones belong to the Pieridae family of butterflies, otherwise known as the Whites and Sulphurs.

The male Brimstone is yellow on the upper side, whilst the female is a paler cream colour. Males have a yellow-green underside, and when they rest with their wings folded, they are camouflaged to look like a young leaf. The female of the species has lighter undersides. They both have a tiny brown spot on each wing. Their angular appearance and predominant veins add to their leaf-like appearance.

Brimstones are large butterflies, with a wingspan of 60mm.

Caterpillars are pale green with a thin white stripe down their sides. They feed on common buckthorn leaves, found in sunny or shady spots on most soils, as well as alder buckthorn, which is located on moist acid soils and wetland. Adults feed heavily on brown knapweed, field scabious and devil's-bit scabious.

They are common throughout the UK, although rare in Scotland, and have seen an increase in numbers of 20% since the 1970s. They favour woodland edges, flowery grassland, meadows, roadside verges, gardens and fenland.

Brown Long-Eared Bat

The brown long-eared bat, *Plecotus auratus*, is also known as the 'whispering bat' due to its quiet vocalisations. It is found throughout Eurasia, in grassland, heath and moorland, orchards, woodlands, towns and gardens, although it is not present in Greece, the south of Italy and Spain.

Its brown ears are nearly as big as its body, and it rolls them back, or tucks them under its wings when dormant. It has a body length of 4.5cm, as well as the tail and forearms, which are both a further 4.2cm. Their oversized ears measure 3.3 to 3.9cm, and make them easy to identify. They are light grey in colour with a paler underside and are similar to the much rarer grey long-eared bat, but smaller. The brown long-eared bat does not fly so quickly as other bat species, maybe due to its large appendices.

It roosts in the roofs of buildings, as well as tree holes and caves, and also uses bat boxes. Like all UK bat species, the brown long-eared bat is nocturnal. Although UK numbers are not known, bats can be best viewed from April to October, flying along the paths of rivers or hedgerows an hour after sunset. However, the loss of woodland is inevitably causing a downturn in numbers, as they rely on this ground to roost and hunt. UK law protects all bat species, making it illegal to disturb, hurt or kill them.

Moths form the majority of their diet. They use their disproportionately large ears and eyes to pick up their invertebrate prey. Their hearing is so acute that they can hear the sound of a moth in flight. They are able to hunt using hearing alone, but also use echolocation to find earwigs, spiders, flies, beetles and other insects in the dark. Gliding slowly, they dive low, even to the ground, to capture their quarry, which they can eat whilst flying, although they tend to hang upside down on their perch to eat bigger prey.

They mate in autumn; however, they can inhibit pregnancy until spring when they congregate in maternal roosts of up to 35 mothers. They give birth to a single pup from late June to July, and these young become independent in six weeks. Throughout November to April, bats take themselves to caves, mines and tunnels to hibernate for the winter. They are hunted by birds of prey and domestic cats.

Bumblebee

There are 276 recorded species of bee in the UK, serving an important role as pollinators of food crops and wildflowers. Theirs is a vital niche in the ecosystem. Social bees include bumblebees, honeybees and the common carder bee. Solitary bees include mason bees, leaf cutter bees, mining bees and carpenter bees. There are more than 25,000 species of bee worldwide, made up of 4,000 genera and 9 families.

More than 250 bumblebee species belong to the genus *Bombus* in the Apidae family. These bees tend to be located in the most northern parts of the world, including the UK. They are not found in Australia, although they have been introduced to Tasmania. They have also been exported to New Zealand, serving as valued pollinators. They do inhabit Africa, north of the Sahara. Bumblebees range in higher latitudes and altitudes than other bees, as they are able to withstand the cold due to their ability to control their own body temperature, including the practice of 'shivering'. Other bees can do this too, but not to the same extent. Classified as social bees, bumblebees create colonies around a single queen. Cuckoo bumblebees, common in Britain, particularly in the south, do not make their own nest. Instead, their queen enters another bee species' nest, killing the host queen and laying her own eggs, which are then tended by the existing workers.

The name, 'bumblebee' was first recorded in 1530 in the UK. It is predated by 'humblebee', documented from 1450, although its usage has declined since the Second World War. The name 'dumbledor' has been used regionally in days of yore, and more recently by J. K. Rowling for her character in the Harry Potter series (1997 to 2007).

Bumblebees are easily recognisable, with plump, furry bodies. They are bigger than honeybees, with a more rounded tip to their abdomen. Their usually bright colouring serves as a warning signal to predators. Divergent species of bumblebee sharing a habitat often look very similar. For example, California has many species of all-black bumblebee, whilst in a different region, all the species are black and yellow. This is an example of Müllerian mimicry and is used to aid defence, as a juvenile predator will get stung once, and leave all the same coloured species alone after that. Another form of Müllerian mimicry is shown by the parasitic cuckoo bumblebee which bears a strong resemblance to the bumblebees that it gets to raise its young.

Batesian mimicry is when a harmless species, such as a hoverfly, takes on the colouration of a species such as a bumblebee in order to fool a predator, which

may have already had a bad experience eating a bumblebee. Batesian mimicry of bumblebees also occurs in robber flies, horseflies, bot or warble flies and bee flies. Their colour can range from all black, to vivid red, orange, yellow, white or pink.

Charles Dickens noted in his *On the Origin of the Species*, published on 24 November 1859: 'From experiments which I have tried, I have found that the visits of bees, if not indispensable, are at least highly beneficial to the fertilisation of our clovers; but the bumblebees alone visit the common red clover (*Trifolium pratense*), as other bees cannot reach the nectar.'

Bumblebees rely on nectar, and have evolved a long, hairy tongue, known as the proboscis, in order to feed. It reaches into tubular flowers, persistently dipping its tongue into the liquid nectar, which is sucked into the mouth. It carries this proboscis, tucked up, under its head whilst travelling. Nectar is collected and stockpiled in the nest, whilst the pollen is taken for the young to eat. Bumblebees are able to navigate using colour and spatial awareness to find the right blooms to enter. Honeybees are in possession of short tongues and therefore tend to feed on open flowers.

Bumblebees are able to cope with weaker light conditions that honeybees, as their furry bristles keep them warm. The length of these fibres increases with latitude. Muscles in the wings need to be 30°C or more to get the bumblebee airborne. Scientists have shown that the action of shivering for five minutes at an air temperature of 13°C is enough to get the bumblebee moving.

As a result, bumblebees can fly at a lower temperature than honeybees or carpenter bees. Chill-coma temperature is the term used for the temperature at which flight insects cannot fly, as their muscles aren't warm enough. The species *B. bimaculatus* has the lowest chill-coma temperature of bumblebees, at 7°C, but it is thought that it can flyer at even lower temperatures than that, out of laboratory conditions, because in nature it would have shelter in which to warm its muscles first.

Honeybees have more stripes than a bumblebee, which may not have any at all. Bumblebees exhibit black fur, whilst the honeybee is a greyer shade. The largest bumblebee in the UK is *B. terrestris*, with massive queens of up to 23mm in length. Her workers are also big, at 16mm, and males are roughly the same. This bee, known as the buff-tailed bee or the large earth bumblebee, is noted as being the most copious bumblebee in Europe. It is used throughout the world for pollination in greenhouses. The largest ever bumblebee, measuring up to 40mm, is the *B. dahlbomii*, found in Chile and known to many as the 'flying mouse'.

Bumblebees lack ears, instead relying on vibrations created by sound. They do not 'dance', as honeybees do, to indicate the direction of food. They will, however, zoom around the nest when back from a feeding trip, and it is thought that they communicate with the vibrations of their wings, to get the other bees out and about. Bumblebees are more likely to go foraging if stockpiles of honey are low.

An interesting study in 2017 got bees moving big objects, for which they were rewarded. The first bees were shown how to do it with a magnet, which they did not quite grasp. Later bees, who had observed the first group, were more capable of completing the task. Researchers realised the importance of social learning within the bumblebee group, but thought that they were not trying to imitate one another precisely, instead mimicking their objectives, leading to the desired result.

The bumblebee's exoskeleton, which supports and protects its body, is segmented. From within the abdomen, wax is produced. This wax is moved by the legs, from the body and sculpted until it softens. The queen produces a lot when she is nesting, as do the younger worker bees. It is used for making the honeycombs and to shield the eggs, as well as to stockpile by coating vacant cocoons.

The bumblebee's scientifically classified tribe, to which its genus, *Bombus*, belongs, is called the *Bombini*. This tribe is said to have been in existence for 25 to 40 million years. Other bee tribes are over double that age. Scientists look at levels of eusociality, in other words, level of social organisation, to determine how different tribes evolved together or separately. Fossil evidence can be difficult to classify.

Colony size depends on the species, but ranges between 50 and 400 bees. This is small in comparison to the honeybee, which forms groups of around 50,000 individuals. Various species nest underground, in old rodent holes, whilst others find homes in long grass or trees. They do not exhibit the neat, hexagonal combs of a honeybee; instead their colonies are more randomly arranged. In temperate zones, these nests only last a year as they cannot withstand the chill of the winter.

THE SECRET LIFE OF AN ARABLE FIELD

At the beginning of spring, the queen locates the right place in which to lay her eggs, building wax cells to deposit them. These eggs would have been fertilised the year before, and will bring forth female workers, who will form the basis of the colony, feeding the young and tending to the nest. In temperate regions, the queen mates in the autumn. She survives the winter, whilst male drones and female workers die. Queens go into diapause, or hibernation, underground, until the weather warms up again.

The sperm, gathered from the males, is stored in the queen's body, and she reproduces according to her needs. A fertilised egg becomes a diploid female, with two sets of chromosomes, one from each parent. She will become a worker bee or a queen, depending on whether her ovaries develop, which is controlled hormonally. An unfertilised egg will turn into a haploid male, i.e. with a single set of chromosomes. The queen produces mainly workers to begin with, as they need to take on the maintenance of the colony. Male bees are born later, as their role in reproduction is not required for some time.

The nest grows in numbers, and by the first or second generation, the queen is still laying her eggs whilst the workers go and look for food. Larvae need both carbohydrates from nectar and protein from pollen. The adults will feed the young, by boring a hole into their brood cells, and pouring in nectar which they carry in their mouths. If the bumblebee species has pollen 'pockets' or 'baskets', they create a store of pollen near the larvae, to which the larvae will help themselves. If the species does not have these pockets, they take on the task of feeding pollen to the larvae individually.

The queen controls the female workers, preventing them from laying eggs using physical domination and pheromones. Female workers are able to give birth to haploid males, and it is only the queen who can give birth to diploid female workers and new queens. Most eggs laid by the workers will be eaten so the queen's line is unbeaten. As the season goes on, the queen finds it harder to stop her workers laying eggs. This competition leads bumblebees to be known as 'primitively eusocial', meaning that workers have retained their ability to reproduce, compared to 'highly eusocial' species, where workers have lost their reproductive options. Most bumblebee species have only one queen per colony; however, there are a few species that will have multiple queens in a colony.

Bumblebees can travel 1 to 2km from their nest, returning to the same group of flowers every day. This is known as flower or pollinator constancy. They can fly at speeds of 15m/s or 34mph, using colour and spatial awareness to choose their pollen source. Electricity in the air seeps into flowers, taking time before it is absorbed by the earth. This is a useful indicator for the bumblebee, who can use it to tell if another bee has been on the flower. Flower temperature is another good gauge. Bumblebees use their long tongue to reach the nectar and can also bite at the base of the flower to get at the nectar in a process known as 'nectar robbing', as they forego their pollination role in doing so.

Usually, bumblebees fly directly into a flower. Their hairy body picks up a good dose of pollen, which is then transferred to the next flower, allowing fertilisation and reproduction. Buzz pollination is a process whereby the flight muscles create movement that scatters the pollen. Queens and workers collect this pollen into their pollen baskets on their back legs, which can each hold up to a million pollen grains. The pollen and nectar are then taken to the nest to either feed to larvae or to stockpile in wax cells. Male bumblebees lack this pollen basket and therefore are more responsible for pollen transfer between plants. Their aim is to retrieve nectar for themselves. As a result of their divergent requirements, they use a vastly different flower stock compared to the female workers. In contrast to honeybees, bumblebees only stockpile food that will last them a few days. They are therefore very prone to changes in the weather or anything that will create a famine.

Bumblebees leave a scent trail on the flowers which impedes other bumblebees from using that flower. It is thought that this scent marks different flowers, sorting them into good nectar sources, and not so good, and allows the bumblebee to see who else has been there. This scent is all the more important on flowers which have a high 'handling' time i.e. flowers in which it takes a long time to locate the nectar.

Bumblebees are able to travel long distances due to their strong flight muscles and wings, which they beat around 200 times every second. Rather than contracting their thorax muscles they vibrate them, allowing them to reach this frequency.

Bumblebees are ones to watch out for, as they don't have barbs on their stings, and therefore do not die if they sting you, since their smooth stings do not get stuck in your skin. Contrastingly, honeybees do have a barb, which they leave in the skin when they sting, and this subsequently kills them. However, bumblebees are not known for their aggression, except in protecting their nest or if threatened. Cuckoo bumblebees exhibit different behaviour. They will be incredibly violent towards their host colony but not attack other animals unless disrupted.

However, the sting is not always effective. Predators such as the badger will unearth and eat an entire nest. Robber flies and beewolves enjoy a tasty dish of bumblebee in North America, whilst in Europe, birds, such as the bee-eater species found in southern Europe, will catch the bumblebee in flight. In the UK, great tits have been observed in the same activity. The crab spider, living in grasslands, woodlands and gardens in the UK, is known to eat bumblebees when they are feeding on flowers. The great grey strike is a bird that finds bumblebees up to 100 metres away, squeezing out the sting by putting pressure on the mandibles. The European honey buzzard trails the bumblebees as they return to their nest and eats all that it finds.

Bumblebees are a host to a variety of parasites which act in differing ways, such as impeding the queen in forming a colony. For example, 12% of bumblebees in the UK have been found to have deformed wing virus. Bee moths are known to lay their eggs in a bumblebee nest so that they can feed on the bumblebee young.

THE SECRET LIFE OF AN ARABLE FIELD

Bumblebees are being recognised for their vital role in pollinating crops and wildflowers, and are being cultivated especially for this purpose. They are uniquely able to pollinate tomato plants, kept under glass, by buzz pollination, a technique that is able to liberate pollen firmly held by the anthers. This practice began in the Netherlands in 1987. There are now 30 bumblebee farms across the globe, mainly using the buff-tailed bumblebee, with more than one million nests produced each year in Europe alone. Some bumblebees have escaped their confines, resulting in injury and disease to native insects. As a result, countries try and farm bees that are indigenous to their surroundings.

Bumblebees prefer the northern hemisphere. New Zealand started growing red clover in the 1800s, but as there were no pollinators, they had to import new seed each year. Between 1885 and 1886, 443 queens were shipped in, and the clover began to flourish. Studies in Canada and Sweden have shown that although bees happily feed off a monoculture, such as oil seed rape, they do a lot better with a variety of crops.

Farming has changed over the years, and it has thoroughly affected the life of the bumblebee. In the 1940s, after the Second World War, horses were still used on the farm. These horses were fed on permanent fields of clover, with a supplement of hay, allowing for wildflower meadows which the bumblebees loved. As time went on, the horses were removed in favour of machinery, and pesticides and fertilisers crept in. The bees suffered as a result. Either they ate the nectar that was infected by these chemicals, or they brushed against it, affecting the health and size of their colony.

Pesticides are causing havoc. One, neonicotinoid, decreased the quantity of new queens by 86%, which has massive implications for the size of future colonies. Even in small amounts, colony size is reduced by 55%, with brain injury to the bumblebees being an outcome, affecting their ability to pollinate and feed.

There were once 19 species of native bumblebee in the UK, and six species of cuckoo bumblebee. Three species have died out completely and eight species are severely threatened. There are only six species that are still found in healthy populations. This will have catastrophic effects on plant pollination. The demise of the bee jeopardises continued human existence.

There are beginning to be serious initiatives to help the bumblebee, including importing some of the short-haired bumblebees from New Zealand, which had been sent over there from the UK over 100 years ago. These have been given an 800-hectare site in Kent, where they are flourishing, with at least five other high priority species of bumblebee. This work is being done by the Bumblebee Conservation Trust. In 2008, the first bumblebee sanctuary in the world was created in Scotland.

Cinnabar Moth

The cinnabar moth, *Tyria jacobaeae*, belongs to the Arctiinae family, and is native throughout Europe and the west and east of Asia. This moth was first recorded by Linnaeus in 1758, where he describes its black wings with red markings, which resemble the red mineral, cinnabar.

Cinnabar moths have a wingspan of 33 to 43mm, with a length of 21mm. They fly by day, and similar to other vividly coloured moths, they are inedible to most species. The larvae tend to feed from *Senecio* plants, especially arrowleaf ragwort, *Senecio triangularis*, in North America. Groundsel, *Senecio vulgaris*, is also popular, but does not give the same survival rates for successive generations. Caterpillars feed on the underside of the leaves, taking in the toxic alkaloids, becoming inedible to many species themselves as they do so. The bright colours of the adult moth, and of the caterpillar, which is black and yellow, serve as a warning to predators, which avoid them. However, cuckoo species are able to consume both the moth and larvae. Ants such as the *Formica polyctena* also eat the caterpillar.

The female cinnabar moth will lay a clutch of 30 to 60 eggs on the ground-facing side of the *Senecio* leaf. When they hatch, the caterpillars feed on the area directly around them, graduating to further leaves and the flowers as they get older. They are known to strip a plant bare, and will turn to cannibalistic behaviour if their food source runs out, or else face starvation. Caterpillars grow up to 3cm.

The cinnabar moth, as well as the ragwort flea beetle, are effective in acting as a biological control agent of ragwort in the US, Australia and New Zealand.

Colorado Potato Beetle

The Colorado potato beetle, *Leptinotarsa decemlineata*, is a headache for potato farmers. It measures 10mm in length and 3mm wide, with a vivid yellow/orange body and 10 strong, brown lines down its elytra – or modified, hardened forewings. Indigenous to America, it found its way to Europe from the 1870s, and has the potential to spread to the temperate regions of Asia, Australia, New Zealand and southern Africa. It was first recorded in 1811, feeding in the Rocky Mountains on the buffalo bur, *Solanum rostratum*. Its ability to destroy potato crops was not noticed until 1859 in Nebraska. By 1875, many European countries stopped the importation of potatoes from America in an attempt to halt its spread; however, the occurrence of the World Wars in Europe prevented the containment of this beetle. It has been eradicated in the UK several times, with the last infestation known in 1976.

Colorado beetles, or Yankee beetles as they are sometimes called, lay more than 500 eggs over a month-long period, with some regions showing over three generations each year. It feeds on the Solanum genus, which as well as potatoes, includes plants like the tomato, pepper, and nightshade species. Predators include the ground beetle, shield bugs, lacewings, wasps, damsel bugs and the Coccinellidae family of beetles, as well as several spiders.

In Michigan, this beetle cost farmers 14% of their income in 1994, as it became resistant to insecticides. The beetle developed a resistance to DDT in 1952, and subsequently to dieldrin in 1958. In total, it has become resistant to 56 insecticides. Rotation of crops has been effective, showing a 95% reduction in early season adults. Mulching the crops increases the density of the beetle's predators.

Comma Butterfly

The comma butterfly, *Polygonia c-album*, breeds throughout western and southern Europe, parts of Asia and north Africa. It is a stunning medium-sized butterfly, with a wingspan of 55 to 60mm. Found throughout the UK, although less common in Scotland and Northern Ireland, it has seen a 58% increase in numbers since the 1970s, even though numbers did fall dramatically in the early twentieth century. It belongs to the Nymphalidae family of butterflies, otherwise known as the Brushfoots.

The comma has an amazing ability to resemble the dead leaves in which it roosts. With its loosely scalloped wings and brown underside, it blends in perfectly. Caterpillars have a black body with white markings behind the neck. They feed mainly on the common nettle, but will also be tempted by hops, elms, willows, rotting fruit and currants (*Ribes spp.*). Due to their camouflage techniques, it is hardly surprising that these butterflies breed in open woodland and woodland edges.

Common Centipede

The common centipede, *Lithobius forficatus*, is one of over 45 centipede species found in the UK. It is found throughout the year, in woodland, farmland, grassland and gardens. It can be difficult to identify due to similarities between species, although this is one of the larger types, measuring 30mm.

It has a thin, reddish-brown body, made up of 15 segments, complete with long antennae. Although some centipedes do have 100 legs, this one actually has 15 pairs, which allows it to walk backwards as well as forwards. The back pair could easily be mistaken for another pair of antennae. It uses these back legs and long antennae to orientate itself, since, as a nocturnal species it does not have good vision.

Hunted by mammals, birds and toads, it feasts itself on spiders, slugs, worms, flies and other insects and invertebrates. By trapping them with its forelegs and injecting them with poison from the claws on its head, it manages to subdue its prey, eating it with its powerful jaws. Hunting by night, they spend the day burrowed in the soil, or hiding in the dark, under stones, dead wood or within a compost heap.

Common Dog-Violet

The common dog-violet, *Viola riviniana*, is found on grassland, farmland, heath and moorland, woodlands and in the garden. It is a small plant, growing up to 12cm high, with pansy-like, five-petalled flowers from April to June. It is unscented, which can differentiate it from other violets, such as the sweet violet, which was used as a scent in classical times. However, the dog-violet is an incredibly important species for a number of fritillary butterflies, who deposit their eggs on the plant.

It is found throughout Europe and in north Africa. Other dog-violets, so named as a derogatory term because they are unscented, include *Viola canina*, *Viola labradorica* and *Viola reichenbachiana*. The common dog-violet is the most widely seen.

Common Rough Woodlouse

The common rough woodlouse, *Porcellio scaber*, is a land-living crustacean that needs cool, dark and damp conditions, as it tends to dry out. It is native to the UK, and is an oval creature, with a grey, uneven exoskeleton, formed by seven segments, each possessing a pair of legs. It measures 15mm in length. The common rough woodlouse occupies every continent, with the exception of Antarctica, having been spread across the world by human movement.

They eat almost everything: leaf litter, dead animals and wood, fungus and fallen fruit, and are even partial to a meal of their own dung. This is a result of the copper present in the dung, and like marine crustaceans their blood is copper based. They feed at night, resting under rocks and dead wood in the daytime. Woodlice are preyed upon by a variety of spiders, birds, frogs and toads, and reptiles.

Females are loving mothers, carrying the eggs in a brood pouch on their underside. Once hatched, the mother stays with the small, white young for several months, until they grow older. She can have as many as three batches of eggs a year, with 25 to 35 eggs in each bundle. A woodlouse can expect to live for two to three years.

It is a known fact that Woodlice cannot urinate, rather emitting an ammonia gas which can build up quite strongly in large groups, leading to the name 'stinky pig'.

Corn Bunting

The corn bunting, *Emberiza calandra*, is the largest of all British buntings. It is also the least decorative. Both sexes have a similar colouring, although the male is 20% larger. They have a length of 18cm, with a wingspan of 26 to 32cm and weigh in the region of 35 to 56g. There are thought to be 11,000 territories in England. Corn buntings resemble larks in their markings, with streaked grey to brown feathering above, and white underbellies, which are also streaked in brown. Their tail is purely brown. They have a fluttering flight, and will hover over the ground, legs dangling, before taking off. Corn buntings are usually found perching on fence posts, undergrowth or electric wires, with the male singing a rapidly repeating note that has been compared to jangling keys.

These birds can be found in England all year round, as well as in southern and central Europe, north Africa and Asia, where they are resident, although they will migrate in colder regions. The corn bunting is very rare in Scotland. They enjoy open land, scattered with trees, particularly favouring farmland and wasteland. They feed on stubble, root crops, weeds, and in cattle yards, flocking in winter. Due to the increase in intensive farming, weeds and insects are becoming scarce, leading to a decline in numbers, particularly in Wales, where the birds were once prolific and are now, sadly, thought to be extinct. Numbers, on average, are down by 90% in the UK, between 1970 and 2007.

Corn buntings feed on seeds, but will eat insects, particularly when looking after their young. Males are very territorial during the breeding season, and will breed with up to three females each, although they do not take a large role in looking after the chicks. The female builds the nest, which is made of grasses and plant stems and lined with rootlets and animal hair. It is usually situated about 1.5 metres above the ground in a hedgerow, or set within a grassy area surrounded by tall plants, such as thistles. Three to five whitish eggs, with strong black/brown lines and spots are laid. The female incubates them for 12 to 13 days, and they will fledge after a further 10 days. The male starts taking an interest in the chicks and begins to feed them when they are half grown.

Corn Marigold

The corn marigold, *Glebionis segetum*, has spread from the Mediterranean to other parts of Europe with very early agriculture, as well as to China and areas in North America. It is commonly known in the UK as corn daisy.

It is an herbaceous perennial, standing 80cm in height, with deeply lobed leaves, which can reach 20cm in length. It produces vivid yellow flowers, which are about 5cm wide, comprising of ray florets circling the disc florets.

Although considered by some to be a pernicious weed, it is highly valuable as a nectar source, ranking alongside the cornflower, *Centaurea cyanus*. This is partly due to its lengthy flowering season, compared with plants such as the bull thistle, *Cirsium vulgare*, which has a high level of nectar sugar, but a short blooming period.

Small butterflies, such as the pearl crescent, and tiny hoverflies, like the Japanese beetle, eat the florets.

The plant has not always been appreciated. Alexander II decreed in Scotland, in the thirteenth century, that if any contamination by even a single plant got into his crops, the farmer would have to pay the penalty of a sheep.

The leaves and young shoots are edible and can be eaten in salads or cooked in oil.

Cornflower

The cornflower, *Centaurea cyanus*, is native to Europe, although it has found its way to North America, Australia and other parts of the world, travelling with crop seeds. It was introduced to the UK as far back as the Iron Age. The cornflower, also referred to as bachelor's button, was once prolific in the cornfields of the UK. Due to herbicide use and intensive agriculture it is now becoming extremely rare. However, it has been domesticated in gardens, where cultivars range in colour from pink to purple.

In the wild, it grows annually to a height of 40 to 90cm, flowering throughout the summer with vivid blue flower-heads that measure 15 to 30mm wide. The flowers can be used to flavour salads, as well as herbal teas. The European goldfinch is particularly partial to cornflower seeds.

It holds a vast array of national significance across the countries of Europe; for example, at the time of Napoleon, where his forces were advancing, Queen Louise of Prussia escaped from Berlin, hiding within a field of cornflowers. She kept her children silent by making garlands with the flowers. At the unification of Germany in 1871, the cornflower became a national symbol.

Cow Parsley

Cow parsley, *Anthriscus sylvestris*, is native to Europe, northwest Africa and western Asia. It belongs to the Apiaceae family, along with others such as the carrot, parsley, hogweed and hemlock. It is found in hedgerows, roadsides, farmland and woodland edges, flowering from April to June, vigorously growing up to 170cm with branching umbrella-like formations of small, white flowers.

Cow parsley enjoys partial shade, and grows through underground rhizomes, as well as producing large numbers of seeds per year. This has led to some parts of the world classifying it as invasive.

Traditionally, cow parsley was used to treat stomach and kidney disorders, as well as respiratory problems. It is an effective mosquito repellent.

It is not to be mistaken for the giant hogweed, *Heracleum mantegazzianum*, which was introduced to Britain in the nineteenth century, often growing near water. This plant causes phytophotodermatitis, blistering and scarring the skin.

Cowslip stems are hollow, and the plant is deciduous. Its leaves resemble ferns, and it attracts a multitude of species, from orange-tip butterflies, which enjoy the nectar, to rabbits, which nibble young leaves. It is a vital source of early pollen for insects.

Cowslip

The cowslip, *Primula veris*, belongs to the primrose family and is found throughout temperate Europe and western Asia. It is not seen in northwest Scotland however, although its presence is felt in Scandinavia. It readily hybridises with other members of the primula family to give plants such as false oxlip (*Primula veris x vulgaris*), a combination of cowslip and primrose.

Primroses prefer partial shade, whilst cowslips favour more open habitats, such as fields, meadows and cliff edges. They are now considered rare, due to the intensive farming that took off in the 1970s and 1980s. The plant is now actively cultivated for seed mixes used for motorway verges.

The cowslip is thought to take its name from its common habitat, that of grasslands where cows were grazing. *Veris*, the species name, comes from the Latin for 'spring'.

Cowslip grows to 25cm in height, with a basal rosette of leaves. Between 10 to 30 beautiful yellow blooms gather on each stem, each one being about 1cm wide.

Cowslip flowers can be used to flavour wine. They were used by the Druids as they enhance the absorption of other herbs.

Crab Apple

The crab apple, *Malus sylvestris*, belongs to the rose family Rosaceae. There are around 30 to 55 small, deciduous trees in the genus, made up of the culinary eating apples, as well as the wild apples. The crab apple contains malic acid, which gives it its bitter taste, and both malic acid and the genus name, *Malus*, are derived from the Latin, *mālum,* meaning 'bad'. They live in temperate regions in the northern hemisphere and are considered native in the UK as they re-established here after the last Ice Age, around 11,700 years ago.

The crab apple will grow anywhere between 2 and 10 metres. It is a spiny, wild tree with white, pink or red flowers from May to June. Although a small tree, it is densely foliaged with large, twisting branches and leaves of 80 to 110mm that are smooth and oval shaped. Fruits are smaller than cultivated apples, at 25 to 30mm. These are yellow-green, with red tinges, widely enjoyed by birds.

Crab apples need to be cross-pollinated by insects, especially bees, which are very attracted to their nectar. Crab apples, like most temperate-climate fruits,

such as apples, blueberries and the majority of plum, cherry and pear trees, are self-sterile. Their pollen does not fertilise their own flowers and they therefore require a compatible variety to cross pollinate them so that they can produce fruit.

Although the fruit is small and hard, with a sharp taste, it is amazing to think that it is the forebearer of all the cultivated apple species that we know today. Careful selection over the centuries has produced a range of wonderful food and drink. Still useful, the crab apple provides a rootstock, generating new varieties, and helping existing varieties to gain beneficial traits, such as the ability to grow in a cold environment.

Due to the malic acid content, crab apple fruit is sour and therefore not eaten raw, although in areas of southeast Asia this bitter fruit is utilised as a condiment when eating chilli or certain fish. Some varieties of crab apple are sweeter, such as the 'Chestnut' cultivar. They all contain a good percentage of pectin, a fibre found in fruits that has strong medicinal qualities, and which can be added to cider to give a distinctive taste. In the past, crab apples were fermented to create a juice known as 'verjuice' which was said to help scalds and sprains. The wood can be carved when it is green. When dry it becomes much harder to fashion. When burnt it emits a pleasant aroma and can be used to smoke foods. It is also good for culinary fires, as it burns at a high temperature, slowly and with minimal flames.

Cutworm

Cutworms are nocturnal moth caterpillars, hiding in the soil by day, and emerging at night to feed on vegetation. By their action of feeding on a stem, they cause it to fall. They create enormous damage to vegetable and cereal crops, sometimes only eating a little of their felled crop before going on the next stem.

Cutworms avoid daylight, as that is when their predators are out. There are various different species, some eating roots, some climbing trees, while others can destroy gardens and fields within days.

They are mostly green, grey, brown or yellow, often with strips down their back, and about 25mm in length. They spend the winter in the soil, which is when farmers can take assertive action, as ploughing kills many of them from exposure and as well as predation by birds. This is especially appropriate for cereal crops and can be a useful tool in the garden too, digging to a depth of 5cm and taking out each cutworm by hand.

Keeping weeds down in winter, thereby removing their food source also helps. Manure and compost applications need to be reduced, in favour of other types of fertiliser. Poisoning the cutworm with a sweetened bran mash is also effective, although care must be taken, by making it fine and lightly scattered, so as not to poison other animals.

Wasps and flies use the cutworm as hosts to lay their eggs, eventually causing death to the caterpillar.

Daisy

The daisy, *Bellis perennis*, belongs to the family Asteraceae. It is found throughout western, northern and central Europe, and has been introduced to North and South America, Australia and New Zealand. There are other plants going by the same common name, so it is differentiated by calling it the lawn or English daisy. In the past, it has been known as bruisewort or woundwort, referring to its medicinal uses. Indeed, Roman soldiers were ordered to pick vast quantities of the flower to extract the juice, which they would then use to soak bandages to wrap around battle scars. The Latin for 'war' is the word *bellum*.

However, the Latin name for daisy is probably derived from the words *bellis*, meaning 'pretty', and *perennis*, meaning 'everlasting'. The English name is thought to have come from 'day's eye', due to the plants habit of closing its flowers at night, or on dull days, when few pollinating insects fly. Chaucer loved the flower and would wake early in the morning to contemplate it, saying that it would 'soften all my sorrow'.

It spreads readily, with underground rhizomes that support the herbaceous, perennial plant. Leaves are oval and sit close to the soil. Flowers are 2 to 3cm in width,

exhibiting white ray florets with yellow disc blooms in the centre. This disc is circled by two rows of green bracts. They are carried on leafless stems, 3 to 10cm in height.

The daisy flowers throughout the summer but can carry on in winter if it is mild enough. The flower often drives gardeners mad, as it resists removal by mowing. However, in a meadow setting it is appreciated for crowding out harmful weeds. Propagation is by seed or division. The plant usually exhibits self-pollination. It enjoys part or full sun and suffers from no known pests or diseases. Ornamental *Bellis* cultivars are available from the garden centre.

Although leaves become more bitter with age, young specimens are edible, either raw or cooked, and are a useful addition to salads. Flowers can also be eaten and can be made into tea or a nutritional supplement. In the seventeenth century, Nicholas Culpepper commented on the respiratory qualities of the daisy, 'boiled in asses milk, it is very effectual in consumptions of the lungs.' It has been traditionally used across Europe to treat gastrointestinal problems.

THE SECRET LIFE OF AN ARABLE FIELD

Dandelion

The common dandelion, *Taraxacum officinale*, is an herbaceous perennial belonging to the Asteraceae family, also known as the Compositae family. It stands out due to its spring flowering: vivid yellow flowers that become spherical balls of tufted seed, known as 'clocks' or 'blowballs' which have been enjoyed by children for centuries, 'telling the time' by counting the number of puffs needed to disperse the seeds. Dandelions are generally considered a weed, growing widely on roadsides and riverbanks, enjoying damp soils and temperate climates. Dandelions have been found in fossils from the Pliocene period in Russia, going back around 2.5 million years.

The word dandelion is derived from the French, 'dent de lion', meaning 'lion's tooth', referring to the serrated edge of the leaves.

The exact taxonomy of dandelion is hard to clarify, especially as a genus, due to its ability to asexually reproduce and its chromosomal arrangement. There are thought to be over 234 subspecies in the UK alone. If you are uncertain if it is a dandelion, the advice is to cut it. A dandelion is the sole member of the Asteraceae family that has a hollow stem.

The dandelion is native to the temperate regions of Asia and Europe, and was introduced to the Americas as a food and medicine crop, probably with the early settlers. Since then, it has spread throughout North and South America, including Canada, as well as Australasia, India and parts of Africa. In some areas they have been classified as a 'noxious weed' due to their invasive nature, causing damage, not just to lawns and sports fields, but also significantly to agricultural crops.

The dandelion produces a strong taproot that supports up to 10 stems, 5 to 40cm in height. Stems either lack hairs completely or have very few. The stems and leaves contain a milky latex. Stems often have a purple tinge, and each holds a sole, bisexual flower head. Typical of the Compositae family, the flower structure brings together many tiny flowers, or florets. These are made up of disc flowers, which are at the centre, and ray flowers, which grow outwards. A dandelion will have 50 to 200 bright yellow/orange florets on a single flower head, which close up at night and in dull weather. When flowering is over, the flower head dries out over a few days, dropping its petals and stamens, the bracts fall backwards and the ball of seeds opens up. These seeds, known as cypselae, are 2 to 3mm in length, with a tuft, or parachute of hair, on each, aiding wind dispersal.

Seeds are blown a few hundred metres from the original plant by the wind. Germination is not cold weather dependant, but seeds do need 2 to 3cm of soil above them to grow. Each plant is capable of producing 5,000 seeds each year, with an overgrown field of dandelions generating in the region of 40 million seeds per acre. These seeds remain viable for years.

Although the dandelion hosts many insects, it reproduces asexually. It is a useful companion plant, attracting beneficial insects and giving off ethylene gas, which aids fruit maturation. Its taproot is valuable as it brings up nutrients from the soil, making them available for shallower rooting plants, increasing the mineral and nitrogen contents in the soil.

Bees do visit the plant for nectar, even though the pollen is not the best around. Bees particularly like dandelions if they are situated near a monoculture, such as fruit, as it adds variation to their nutritional intake. A large number of caterpillars feed on the dandelion, including the giant leopard moth (in the Americas), the riband wave, small fan-footed wave, the orange swift, grey chi, flame, shark, nutmeg, satellite, gothic, large yellow underwing, setaceous Hebrew character and the tortrix moth – all in Europe. Their speedy spring flowering makes them a useful plant for early emerging butterfly larvae, such as the pearl-bordered fritillary.

The plant has been used for centuries in the kitchen and as a medicine. The word 'officinalis' comes from medieval Latin, denoting plants that were used for this

purpose, referring to the 'officina' or storeroom of a monastery where medicines were kept. Linnaeus intentionally used this term as a specific epithet in 1735 when he published the first edition of *Systema Naturae* to refer to plants that were used for culinary or medicinal use.

The diuretic effect of the plant's roots is shown in its folk name, 'piss-a-bed', reflected in the French, 'pissenlit'. Pollen can be responsible for allergic reactions when consumed, and occasionally contact dermatitis is caused by contact with the latex in the stem and leaves.

Dandelion wine is made from the flowers. Older leaves can be cooked to create a soup, younger leaves can be added raw to salads, and the roots can be baked and ground, making a good alternative to decaffeinated coffee. Uncooked leaves taste a little bitter. They contain high levels of beta-carotene, vitamins A, C and K, with greater levels of iron and calcium than spinach. Dandelion and burdock mead has been drunk in the UK since the Middle Ages, although nowadays it has been made into a soft drink. Dandelion flower jam is very popular across Europe, and the plant has been used in herbal medicine for centuries in Europe, China and by the Native Americans, as well as by the Ancient Greek, Egyptian and Roman cultures. The flowers yield a yellow dye when dried and ground into a powder. Roots are best harvested in April, which is when the plant is beginning to grow again after the winter. All parts of the plant can be eaten, although the seeds are not particularly pleasant. However, due to the high levels of oxalates in the leaves, moderate quantities are ok, but large amounts should be avoided.

Research is being carried out into making rubber, including car tyres, from the latex present in dandelion stems and leaves.

Docks and Sorrels

The docks and the sorrels are species in the *Rumex* genus and are generally regarded as herbs. They grow throughout the world and can be utilised for their edible leaves. They are upright plants, with long taproots, with leaves forming a basal rosette and insignificant flowers clustering above. These blooms tend to be green; however, sheep's sorrel shows brick red flowers and stems.

Over the years, the plants have been utilised for many purposes; for example, broad-leaved dock has big enough leaves to enclose and preserve butter. A dock found in the North American deserts, commonly known as tanner's dock, is used for leather tanning and dying, aided by its roots, which comprise 25% tannin.

Docks and sorrel leaves are edible, containing oxalic acid, which gives them an acidic taste. They exhibit high levels of vitamin A and C, iron and potassium. Older leaves should not be eaten as they are too bitter. Due to large amounts of oxalic acid,

curled dock should not be eaten during lactation as it encourages laxation in the child. *Rumex* species are used for different medicinal purposes throughout the world, as well as widely used as foodstuff. In France, a classic nouvelle cuisine national dish is salmon escalope in sorrel sauce. In the UK, they also play a valuable role in the relief of nettle stings. Helpfully, they usually grow in the same location as the nettles.

The curled dock, *Rumex crispus*, grows to 1 metre high. Brown seeds are contained by the calyx or seed pod, giving them the ability to disperse buoyantly on water, or on the fur of a mammal. This species has a number of subspecies, which thrive in different locations, such as *Rumex crispus* ssp. *crispus* which enjoys wasteland. *Rumex* species are happy to hybridise with other members of the genus.

Curled dock also grows well in meadows and roadsides. It is considered invasive in some parts of the world, including North America and New Zealand, where it makes its way by mingling with crop seeds. The UK pronounced it as an 'injurious weed' in the Weeds Act of 1959. However, it does have its uses. It is the perfect plant for many butterflies and moths, who deposit their eggs on its closely packed leaves that are well placed near the ground.

The roots of curled dock have high levels of iron and are often used with stinging nettles to treat anaemia. Roots and leaves are mild laxatives, but in some cases can cause intestinal soreness. This results from the anthraquinone glycosides in the plant, which have also been the subject of research into cancer treatment.

Dog Rose

The dog rose, *Rosa canina*, is a deciduous, climbing, wild rose found in Europe, northwest Africa and western Asia. It is thought to have got its name in ancient times when the root was used to treat dog bites. Even as late as the nineteenth century, the plant was used in this way with rabid dogs.

It climbs 1 to 5m in height, making its way up through tree branches, helped by its tiny prickles. Blooms are usually pale pink, although they can range in colour from deep pink to white. They have five petals and they form deep red/orange hips once mature.

The hips have high levels of vitamin C, and are used to make jam, tea and syrup. They were widely used in the Second World War as Britain was not able to import citrus fruits, and the government approved the collection of hips to make up for vitamin C deficiency. They were also valued for their ability to cure viral infections, kidney and urinary tract problems. Hips help with arthritis, gout and fevers, while petals aid digestion. During the Vietnamese War, soldiers smoked the plant to help blot out their hunger and fear.

Dog rose is useful in stabilising soil, but it can be incredibly invasive. The plant is used as a root stock for grafting roses. Birds love the rose hips, and aid in seed dispersal.

Earthworm

T he earthworm is found all over the world, usually soil-dwelling, although species of earthworm can be found in rotting wood, mudbanks and even trees, eating both living and dead organic matter. Like other invertebrates, they lack a skeleton, instead maintaining their shape with internal fluids that act to give them a hydrostatic skeleton. Their body is composed of segments, visible by the furrows along their length. The number of segments depends on the species, and all are present in the young when they are born. Each segment is covered with a thin cuticle, coloured red or brown, allowing the passage of mucus, which keeps the worm lubricated, helping it to move through the earth. Beneath this skin is the nervous system and muscular layers.

Worms react to human touch by squirming, as a reaction to the salt on the person's skin, which is toxic to the worm. It is also a pressure response that protects the worm from danger, i.e. from an attack by a bird. Earthworms lack eyes and instead rely on photosensitive cells. The worm's digestive system comprises of a straight tube, running from its mouth to its anus. The worm also lacks respiratory organs, instead exchanging gases through its skin and blood vessels, which is how they take up water and salts as well. Earthworms move by a process of peristalsis, which is the constriction and relaxation of muscles, creating their characteristic wave like movements. The constricted part is held in place on the soil by the bristly hairs set along its length. Soil is excavated with the help of moisturising mucus which is exuded from the body.

The worm is born a smaller version of the adult, only lacking in reproductive organs, which develop in two to three months. It takes a year for them to grow to their full adult size. They are thought to live four to eight years in the field, but in the garden this is reduced to less than two years. Worms are hermaphrodites, containing both male and female reproductive organs. They mate on the surface, usually after dark. There is a transfer of sperm between the two worms. Each worm then emits a substance to create a ring, into which they shoot their own eggs and the introduced sperm. Once they have done this, they withdraw and the ring closes up to form a cocoon in which the foetal worms mature.

There are thought to be about 7,000 species of earthworms in different regions of the world. They are very difficult to classify. Only around 160 species are found world-wide. These are known as cosmopolitan earthworms. Worms are generally

classified as to their environment: leaf litter/compost earthworms, top/sub-soil earthworms and deeply burrowed earthworms. Population numbers depend on a variety of factors, including soil pH, texture, moisture, temperature and aeration levels, with different species thriving in diverse conditions. Earthworms are prone to attack from a wide range of birds, mammals like hedgehogs, moles and foxes, and invertebrates, such as beetles, slugs and snails.

Nitrogenous fertilisers are deadly to the earthworm, as they cannot take the resultant acidic environment. Not only that, but these chemicals travel up the food chain. In Australia, this has led to the government categorising the giant Gippsland earthworm as a protected species. The use of synthetic fertilisers rather than organic methods have seen the extinction of three species globally, with many more at risk. In the garden the earthworm population can be increased by using organic compost on the surface, which gives them the nutrients that they need to flourish.

The earthworm provides an important role in aerating the soil, allowing nutrients to mineralise and increasing their absorption by crops and other plants. Biologically, earthworms use organic matter, such as fallen leaves, to create humus, shredding the leaves, thereby mixing them with the soil. The worm ingests soil, up to 1.25mm in particle size, excreting the casts as nutrient banks for plants. These casts are much richer than the top 15cm of soil in nitrogen (5x), phosphates (7x) and potassium (11x). Each worm is capable of producing 4.5kg of casts annually. Physically, the worm perpetuates the structure of the soil by its burrowing, which creates channels for air and water.

The fertility of soil can be measured by the volume of organic matter blended into it. Charles Darwin summed it up when he said in 1881: 'It may be doubted whether there are many other animals which have played so important a part in the history of the world, as have these lowly organised creatures.'

There are thought to be between 250,000 and 1.75 million earthworms per acre, depending on the quality of the soil. As an acre is 4047m², that makes up to 432 earthworms per square meter, and works out as 7 million earthworms for each human being. There is a global market for earthworms, with 370 million worms sold to the US in 1980, retailing at $54million.

Earthworms are rich in protein and used to be served as a delicacy to Māori chiefs in New Zealand.

Elder

The elder, or elderberry, *Sambucus nigra*, is a member of the family Adoxaceae. It used to be grouped with the honeysuckle family, but was moved after genetic research and morphology pointed it into its new family.

The purple/black berries are what really make the plant stand out. These contain a large percentage of anthocyanidins and are composed of 80% water, 18% carbohydrates, 1% protein and 1% fat. Berries have a high level of vitamin C, with a 100-gram quantity providing 43% of the Daily Value (DV) needed. Other nutrients include an average level of vitamin B (18% DV) and iron (12% DV).

There are, however, warnings. Berries that have been cooked are safe, but uncooked berries, leaves, roots, flowers and stems can be dangerous to health, as they produce

poisonous cyanogenic glycosides. These can cause nausea and vomiting as well as stomach pain and diarrhoea. The berries contain less of this toxic substance than the leaves or flowers. Parts of the tree are used as teas or capsules to treat ailments such as flu, colds and constipation. Not enough research has been done to catalogue its usefulness.

The tree will grow almost anywhere. It is not fussy about soil type or pH, but it does like a lot of nitrogen. It can be found throughout the northern hemisphere in temperate to subtropical areas, but in the southern hemisphere it is limited to regions in South America and Australasia. Ornamental varieties of the elder include *S. canadensis* and *S. racemosa*. Elder is known as an 'instant hedge' as it grows quickly and is simple to shape. It provides a home for a great deal of wildlife.

Lepidoptera species (butterflies and moths) that feed on the elder include the emperor moth, the V-pug moth, swallow-tailed moth, engrailed moth, dot moth, brown-tail and buff ermine moth.

Elderflower syrup is produced in central Europe from the blossoms, and berries are used to make pies and relishes. Socată is a soft drink made in Romania in late spring, where elderflowers are soaked in a mixture of water, yeast and lemon for a few days. Elderflower cordial is created using the flowers of *S. nigra*, whilst the French use these elderflowers to produce the liqueur St-Germain.

Other uses of the tree involve using hollowed-out twigs as spiles to remove syrup from maple trees. Watchmakers also utilise the pith to polish their equipment before work. 'Elderberry juice' is a certified colour used in organic food production. The red colouration derived from the berries is used to colour other goods, such as fibres.

Fallow Deer

The fallow deer, *Dama dama*, belongs to the Cervidae family. It is a ruminant, which describes an even-toed ungulate mammal that chews the cud that it regurgitates from its rumen (or its first stomach).

The word 'fallow' describes the pale brown coat of the deer, whilst '*dama*' has roots in the Latin word '*domo*', meaning 'tame'.

Whilst being indigenous to Europe, fallow deer have been widely introduced around the world; to Argentina, South Africa, Morocco, Tunisia, Algeria, Cyprus, Israel, Australia, Lebanon, New Zealand, the United States, Canada, the Falkland Islands and Peru.

Much of this importation has been carried out with the aim of increasing hunting opportunities in the receiving nation, although in Greece, depictions of the buck and doe fallow deer have been given the honour of replacing the sculpture of the Colossus of Rhodes at the entrance to Rhodes harbour, unveiled in 1947.

The Romans were the first to introduce the fallow deer throughout Europe. Initially the general feeling in the UK was that the Normans had bought them over, and it was not until fallow deer remains were recently found at Fishbourne Roman Palace that it was realised that the Romans introduced them in the first century AD.

Fallow deer now occupy habitats in lowland Britain, roughly south of a line between Norwich and Birmingham, many escaping from parkland. The New Forest and the Forest of Dean, both ancient royal forests of William the Conqueror and Tudor kings, contain historic herds.

They can also be found in Scotland, in Strathtay and Loch Lomond, and surveys suggest that they are increasing their number and territory throughout Britain. The 'long-haired' fallow deer of Mortimer Forest on the Shropshire/Herefordshire border in England exhibit greater tufted ears and more extensive body hair. A large herd of about 450 deer can be found in Phoenix Park in Dublin, where they have been hunted from the 1660s.

Fallow deer are noticeably sexually dimorphic among deer species, with bucks being much larger than does. Bucks measure 140 to 160cm in length, standing 85 to 95cm at the shoulder, and weigh between 60 to 100kg. Female statistics are smaller: 130 to 150cm long, 75 to 85cm high and a weight of 30 to 50kg. Fawns measure 30cm at birth and weigh 4.5kg. They live for 12 to 16 years.

Colour varies, the most common being chestnut with white spots that are more obvious in summer and less so in winter. The rear end is pale, with the tail edged and

THE SECRET LIFE OF AN ARABLE FIELD

striped in black. Other colourations include menil, where spots are seen all year round with no black marking on the tail. Melanistic or black coats are rare; the coat shows as grey-brown to black, lacking spots or white markings. For some reason, there are quite a few melanistic individuals in New Zealand. Finally, and even more unusual, is the leucistic or white, not to be confused with albino. Fawns are a shade of cream, growing up into pure white adults, with no spots. Eyes and noses are dark.

Does do not have antlers – only the bucks. Until they reach the age of three, these antlers will be short spikes. They mature into large, broad, palmate shapes, which they use for fighting during the rutting season. Fallow deer can maintain a speed of 30mph in short spurts. Roe deer can run faster, being better built. Fallow deer can use their skills to jump heights of 1.75 metres and 5 metres wide.

The breeding season is in late October in the northern hemisphere, whilst deer in the south will mate in April. Deer exhibit lekking, whereby males will gather in different spots around the breeding territory, allowing the females to choose between them. The doe will only enter a buck's space if she intends to mate with him. Other breeding strategies, such as harems, temporary stands and dominance groups are shown, but leks are by far the most common.

Before mating, the buck will lick and sniff the doe's backside to see if she is fertile. The buck will emit a shrill whine to signify that he is ready, whereupon the female allows him to mount her, with it all being over in a matter of minutes.

Habitat conditions obviously have a bearing on herd size. Fallow deer feel most at home in woods, where they enjoy dispersed regions of grass, trees and other vegetation. Does and bucks do not spend much time together. They only really meet for the mating season. Bucks will do all they can to occupy the best territory for the rut and they will cease feeding in order to defend this area from other males, losing up to 17% of their weight. Their liver will start to suffer from steatosis, or fatty liver, but this is a reversible condition. If there are many bucks in the same area, some will share the same rutting space.

Fawns are born after a 245-day gestation period. Twins are uncommon. Both genders are sexually mature at 16 months. Mothers like to hide their young in sheltered caves or bushes, where they will lick them all over to get rid of the birthing fluid. Bucks do not take part in looking after the fawns.

The mother will stay away from the herd for a good 10 days after birthing. She will spend limited time with her fawn, only visiting it to feed it for about four hours a day for the first four months. The ability to ruminate is important in the fawn's development, with the fawn being able to do this at the age of two to three weeks. This is closely followed by weaning, which is completed 20 to 30 days later, allowing the fawn and mother to return to the herd. By 12 months the fawn is considered to be an independent creature.

Males do have to fight for their females. Males with larger antlers tend to achieve a greater mating success, especially when these antlers are symmetrical. Antlers that grow more quickly on young bucks tend to lead to a bigger display when they are older. Does will selectively choose a larger male.

Bucks are aggressive at certain times, namely when trying to attract a mate, and when food sources or territorial range are limited. It has been shown that bucks with intact antlers, i.e. they have not been previously damaged, are more likely to be more aggressive in a fight, jumping, clashing or forcing the other buck backwards, but it has also been shown that a buck with damaged antlers usually wins the fights.

THE SECRET LIFE OF AN ARABLE FIELD

Fescues

Fescues are flowering tufted grasses, both evergreen and perennial, growing from 10 to 200cm in height. They have a complex taxonomy. There are thought to be 400 to 500 species within the genus *Festuca*, which belongs to the family of grasses, Poaceae, which incorporates over 10,000 species in all. Fescues are found throughout the world, with the exception of Antarctica. Genetic differences have meant that taxonomists have moved some fescues into the ryegrass genus: *Lolium*. Classifications have been going on since Pliny the Elder, the Roman naturalist, who used the Latin word *festuca*, meaning 'stem' to describe the species. Since then others, such as Linnaeus, have tried to organise the assortment of grasses, with varying degrees of success. Taxonomists these days are concerned with characteristics such as ovary pubescence and arrangement of intercellular tissues when defining genera.

Fescues such as red fescue, *F. rubra*, and Chewing's fescue, *F. rubra* subsp. *Commutate*, are a popular choice for lawns. Other species, such as hard fescue, *F. trachyphylla*, and tall fescue, *F. arundinacea*, are favoured for sports grounds, parks and recovering deforested land. Indeed, a cultivar of tall fescue, 'Kentucky 31', was utilised to

rejuvenate the region after the disastrous Dust Bowl in the 1930s in the US. Tall fescue is reputedly the grass growing on the South Lawn of the White House in Washington.

A great many fescues spread through their rhizomatous or stoloniferous root systems. However, tall fescue reproduces by the process of tillering, where multiple side shoots grow from the initial seedling creating a plant with dense tufts and multiple seed heads. Although not all of these shoots are fertile, it is thought that a pound of seeds in weight approximates to 228,000 individual seeds. Dry soils affect the growth of tall fescue, as roots grow deeper and more sparsely. Temperature also affects the plant and it fails to grow when the soil is less than 4°C. The most prevalent cultivar of tall fescue used agriculturally in the UK is 'S170', which can withstand drought and overgrazing due to its mutually symbiotic relationship with the fungus *Neotyphodium coenophialum*.

However, there is a flip side to this coin. Tall fescue can cause miscarriage in horses, leading to the death of the mare and/or foal. This is due to the presence of alkaloids formed by the endophyte *Epichloë coenophiala*, which lives inside the fescue. Birthing problems such as abortion, stillbirths or prolonged pregnancy result, often with a retained placenta and loss of milk production. These issues tend to start two to three months before birth and the brood mare should be taken off the pasture for this period.

Cattle too suffer from 'fescue toxicosis' as a result of tall fescue, showing symptoms of a rough summer coat and inability to withstand the heat. They take to the shade and utilise water in order to cool down. They may not gain the required weight, experience reduced conception rates, lower milk yields and fat necrosis – which can lead to acute pancreatitis. 'Fescue foot' can occur in winter, when vasoconstriction prevents blood flow to the foot, causing gangrene and lameness. Giving cattle and horses alternative food, such as legumes, as well as the grass, will reduce these effects.

THE SECRET LIFE OF AN ARABLE FIELD

Field Vole

The field vole, *Microtus agrestis*, is thought to number 75 million in the UK alone, although it is absent from Ireland. Field voles are spread throughout Europe, from the Atlantic coast to Lake Baikal in Russia, living in damp, grassy habitats, such as woodland, hedgerows, farmland, heath and moorland. They can thrive in altitudes up to 1,700m.

The field vole is 8 to 12cm in length, with a 3 to 4cm long tail, weighing in the region of 25 to 50g and with a life expectancy of just 1 year. They are grey-brown in colour, with a greyer underbelly.

The field vole is also known as the short-tailed vole. As a result, they are not proficient at climbing. Instead, they use a network of runs through tall plants to

get to their shallow burrows situated under leaf litter and even snow, although they frequently build their nests on ground level in a mound of grass or sedge. They are very tidy mammals and tend to leave their dung in a specific area.

The field vole eats plant matter such as grasses, herbs, tubers and moss, sometimes supplementing this with insect larvae. It particularly favours *Agrostis spp.* and *Festuca rubra* grasses, clover, dandelion, buttercups and yarrow. They are not tempted by tufted hairgrass or rosebay willowherb.

Every year a female field vole with have between three to six litters, with up to four to six young in each. She breeds throughout the year, even in the snow. The gestation period is three weeks, and pups take fourteen days to wean. The male at this time produces a very dense, unpalatable smell, and will defend his territory to the death.

Field voles are a very important food source for barn owls, kestrels and weasels, and they are also preyed on by other owls, stoats, foxes and snakes. They do not hibernate during cold spells, and there are peaks and troughs in population numbers, due to lack of food supplies over winter. By spring, numbers are buoyant; however, food resources become less digestible in mid-summer and numbers drop off again.

Foxglove

The common foxglove, *Digitalis purpurea* belongs to the plantain family, Plantaginaceae. The genus, *Digitalis*, is made up of around 20 species, which are found in Europe, western Asia and the northwest of Africa.

The first documented instance of the name foxglove was by Leonhard Fuchs in 1542 who also named the *Fuchsia* genus. His surname in German literally means 'fox'. There are several theories about the 'glove' reference. Many think that it comes from the Latin name, *digitalis*, or 'finger', perhaps acknowledging the shape of the flower, which grow big enough to contain a finger. In the mid-1800s, other names, such as folk's glove or fairy's glove were put forward by the scientist Henry Fox Talbot; whilst R. C. A Prior proposed foxes-glew, or fairy music. Needless to say, the flowers had certainly caught the romantic imagination, with folk tales of foxes wearing magical gloves to aid them in their hunting.

The species does well in acid soils, enjoying light to deep shade. It favours woodland, moors, heathland, cliffs, banks and mountain sides.

The foxglove flowers every two years. The leaves form a closely grouped circle just above the ground in the initial year. They then spiral round the stem, measuring 10 to 35cm in length and 5 to 13cm in width. They can be mistaken for comfrey (*Symphytum* species) due to the surface texture of their woolly leaves, which are covered with grey/white hairs. Comfrey is traditionally used as a tea, and great care should be taken, as all parts of the foxglove are extremely poisonous.

The stem grows to 50 to 250cm in the second year, with 20 to 80 tubular, pendent flowers forming in early summer along its length. The flowers are characteristically purple, although cultivars of yellow, pink or white can be found. Bees are attracted to the spotted design of the flower's inner tube, which leads the way to the nectar source. Seeds are tiny, at 0.1 to 0.2mm, and they are contained within a capsule.

All parts of the plant, including the root and seed, contain the poisonous cardiac glycoside, digitoxin. It was the British physician William Withering (1741 to 1799) who first documented the use of extracts of foxglove to treat dropsy (edema), which is related to heart failure. It is used today to increase cardiac contractility and act as an antiarrhythmic, controlling heart rate, useful in irregular atrial fibrillation. The active component of foxglove, digitalin, is taken from leaves in the second year of growth.

Historically, digitalis was used to treat seizures, including epilepsy. Nowadays this practice has stopped, due to the side effects of vomiting, nausea, diarrhoea, yellow and blurred vision (with blue halos around lights), heart rate fluctuations, seizures, hallucinations and in extreme cases, death. Van Gogh suffered from seizures and it is thought that his 'Yellow Period' was a result of digitalis therapy. Herbalists don't use foxglove, due to the narrow range of benefits, as well as the extreme care needed in preparing a dose. Even ingesting the water from a jug of the flowers can be fatal to a child, leading to its more sinister name of 'witch's glove'.

However, the plant does play its part in the eco-system. The foxglove pug is a moth which feeds on the flowers of the plant, with the lesser yellow underwing moth enjoying the leaves, amongst other lepidoptera (butterfly and moth) species.

Fruit Fly

There are some 500 different species of fruit fly. The common fruit fly, *Drosophila melanogaster*, came from Africa and is now found all over the world, including islands. They are not officially a 'pest', although they do tend to inhabit human environments. As they do not transmit disease, they are basically harmless. Whilst other fruit flies are more perilous, this species does not induce fruit to rot, but rather it utilises previously rotting fruit.

Common fruit flies are a yellowish brown with red eyes and black stripes across their backs. Females are bigger than males, at 2.5mm, and males are darker in colour. They develop in response to temperature. The quickest maturation of egg to adult takes place at 28°C, taking seven days to develop. At higher and lower temperatures, eggs take longer to develop, with 11 days being common at 30°C, and more than 50 days at 12°C. If eggs are too cramped, resulting flies will be smaller.

Mating takes 20 minutes to complete, with several hundred 1.8mm long sperm injected into the female. The female has many partners, with the final male thought to cause 80% of the offspring. The female lays around 400 eggs into decaying fruit, mushrooms or sap. It only takes 8 to 12 hours for a female to reach sexual maturation once she has emerged.

The fruit fly is utilised widely in the laboratory. It has many advantages: taking up little space and equipment; being easily anesthetised; its body is simple to understand; many generations can be studied over a short period of time; females are very prolific in their egg laying; genders are sexual dimorphic making them easy to differentiate; its complete genome has been sequenced-among other reasons. The fruit fly is particularly useful in genetic and developmental biology research, and by 2017, eight Nobel prizes had been awarded for ground-breaking work using this species.

Garden Spider

The garden spider, *Araneus diadematus*, also known as the cross spider, has a widespread distribution. It favours grassland, heath and moorland, farmland, coastal areas, wetlands, woodlands, towns and gardens. These spiders are large, at 10 to 18mm, and create the most wonderful silky webs, which can be up to 40cm wide. They are seen from June to November building these spiral webs, joined with radial threads. The silk they produce has admirable qualities of not only being incredibly light, but also very strong.

The spider acts by waiting in the middle of the web until it feels the vibrations of an insect on it. It thereupon moves quickly to its prey and captures it in silk, giving it a poisonous bite to finish it off. It stores the insect for later consumption. Flying insects, such as wasps, butterflies and flies are primary targets. The spider itself is prone to predation by birds.

The garden spider can be easily identified by its grey-brown-red colour and the large white cross on its abdomen, made up of smaller spotting and markings. Males are half the size of the female and lead a dangerous life as often they are eaten by the female after mating. The young produced live in a silken egg cocoon until the following spring. The mother will not leave these eggs and looks after them until the autumn when she dies of cold.

Gatekeeper Butterfly

The gatekeeper butterfly, *Pyronia tithonus*, belongs to the subfamily Satyrinae, part of the Nymphalidae family. It is also known as the hedge brown butterfly. The gatekeeper butterfly is common throughout the south and east of the UK, as well as coastal areas in the south of Ireland. Climate change bringing warmer summers has allowed the population to creep further north, and a 50% increase in numbers is expected by 2080 for this reason.

It has similar markings to the meadow brown butterfly if you are looking at their underwings, but the gatekeeper can be distinguished by its double pupils on its forewing eyespots and the fact that it is smaller and slightly more orange than the meadow brown. These eyespots are a deterrent against predation by birds and are so effective that the gatekeeper feels safe enough to rest with its wings open, whereas the meadow brown tends to keep its closed.

The male gatekeeper butterfly has scent scales on his wings, which emit pheromones to attract females. These scales, known as androconia, are located on the dark markings on the upper surface of the forewing. Overall, females tend to have more

spots on their wings. The female is larger than the male. They have a wingspan of around 4.5cm compared to 4cm for the male.

The gatekeeper butterfly lives in a variety of areas, favouring rough grassland, woodland tracks, country lanes, field margins and hedgerows. Like other members of its subfamily, Satyrinae, larvae feed on grasses such as smooth meadow grass (*Poa pratensis*), rough meadow grass (*Poa trivialis*) and sheep's fescue (*Festuca ovina*). Caterpillars vary in colour between green and brown. They pupate in a thin chrysalis which is attached either to the grass or is lying on the ground. The emerging adult butterfly enjoys the fruit of blackberries, whose short flowers suit its small proboscis. They also feed on carline thistles, fleabane, ragwort, wild privet, water mint, wild marjoram, wood sage, thyme and scabious.

The gatekeeper butterfly tends to spend a lot of time in flight but does not cover a great distance. This behaviour can result in a high density of population in one area, but a low density not far away. Most of the time in the air is spent by males finding mates. As a protandrous species, where the males reach sexual maturity before the females, there is only time to breed once, and subsequently there is just one generation of gateway butterflies a year. Adults begin to show in July and their life cycle is over by the end of August. Mating itself lasts around an hour, with butterflies staying still with their wings shut. The female will deposit 100 to 200 eggs, either in a shady spot or by releasing them into the air. These will hatch after 14 days with caterpillars hibernating from September to March. They attain full growth by late May to early June, when they pupate into adults.

Goat Moth

The goat moth, *Cossus cossus*, is our heaviest native moth, found in scattered locations throughout the British Isles. It is considered nationally scarce. It belongs to the Cossidae family of leopard and goat moths, which tend to inhabit riverbanks, marshes, hedgerows, woodland edges, parks and gardens. It is named as such, as the caterpillar smells rather like a goat. The moth is grey in colour, with black and white markings that blend in with tree bark. They have a huge wingspan of 90mm and do not feed as adults.

Caterpillars tunnel holes in the trunks of broadleaf trees, such as oak or ash. They favour damp conditions and can also be found in willow, poplars, birch, alder, apple and other species of fruit tree. The caterpillar eats the wood, emitting waste and fermented sap from its burrow. This sap attracts other insects such as the red admiral butterfly. Caterpillars grow to 100mm in length. They are mahogany red, with deep orange sides and a black head. It takes up to five years for them to develop into an adult, overwintering three to four times as larva, before dropping to the ground to pupate in a soil cocoon in late summer. They begin their adult life the following year in mid-summer. Predators include birds and small mammals.

Goldfinch

The European goldfinch, *Carduelis carduelis*, is found throughout Europe, north Africa and the west of Asia, as well as the Americas, New Zealand and Australia, where they have been widely introduced. The Carduelinae subfamily to which it belongs contains 141 species, and itself is part of the finch family, Fringillidae.

Goldfinches flock in numbers of up to 40, known as a 'charm' due to their dancing flight and pretty song whilst feeding on the seeds of annual weeds, such as thistle or groundsel. Their specialist beaks enable them to access these seeds.

An adult male exhibits a red face and black and white head, with brown/buff back feathers. His tail is black and he shows a white rump, with the distinctive golden yellow bar on black wings. Females share the same colouration with less red on the face. Juveniles are a dull grey, but still have the bright yellow wing design.

Whilst Linnaeus introduced the Latin name for the bird in his tenth edition of *Systema Naturae* in 1758, the English name, 'goldfinch' was first recorded in the late fourteenth century by Geoffrey Chaucer in *The Cook's Tale*, where he states, 'Gaillard

he was as goldfynch in the shawe', which translates to, 'Gaily dressed he was as is a goldfinch in the woods.'

There are many subspecies of the goldfinch, adapted to different parts of their range. They originated in the Miocene-Pliocene period, over 5 million years ago. The goldfinch enjoys open farmland, parkland and gardens, displaying scattered trees and bushes, and will migrate in the colder regions of its range. The majority of birds over-winter in the UK, but some will travel south as far as Spain. They are found throughout the British Isles, apart from the Scottish Highlands, and are most common in the south of England.

The female constructs the cup-shaped nest, situated several metres above ground in small trees or bushes, using moss and lichen, lined with thistle down or other soft material. Four to six white eggs with chestnut brown speckles are laid, and incubated by the female for 11 to 13 days. The male feeds her during this time, and both parents rear the emerging chicks by regurgitating seeds and insects. They fledge after 13 to 18 days, and are fed for a further week. Two to three broods are expected each year.

In the nineteenth century, goldfinches were widely kept in captivity. The RSPB, founded in 1889, did much to halt this practice in the UK. If goldfinches are caged with canaries, they begin to imitate their call, losing their own. Happily, there has been a 64% increase in goldfinch numbers in the UK from 1970 to 2007. Goldfinches particularly love the oil-rich niger seeds on the bird table, which come from the yellow ramtil plant, indigenous to Ethiopia.

Green Hairstreak Butterfly

The green hairstreak, *Callophrys rubi*, is a small butterfly, with a wingspan of 27 to 35mm. It belongs to the Lycaenidae or gossamer-winged family of butterflies, which is the second largest butterfly family, comprised of over 6,000 species globally. Although it is not considered threatened in the EU, numbers in the UK have fallen by 30% in the last 50 years.

Unless it is flying, it will hold its wings together, exhibiting a bright, leafy green underside, with a broken white stripe, varying in extent. It has faintly scalloped wings, which are tinged in brown and white. The upper side of the wings are brown, with darker veins. Males have a scent patch on their forewings; a tiny tube-shaped structure, emitting smells to attract mates. Scent patches also release heat, which is vital on hot, sunny days.

Caterpillars feed on chalky grassland plants such as rock-rose and bird's foot trefoil. On heathland, gorse is popular, as is broom and Dyer's greenweed. Moorland plants, like bilberry, are enjoyed, whilst shrubs such as buckthorn, dogwood, heath and bramble are also favoured.

This widespread abundance of food creates many habitats for the butterfly, including chalk grassland, scrubland, heaths, meadows, open grassland and woodland edges. The butterfly is rarely seen in gardens.

Greenfinch

The greenfinch was a success story, with numbers growing in the UK by 23% between 1970 and 2007. There are ten recognised subspecies of greenfinch, *Carduelis chloris*, found throughout Europe and Asia, as well as north Africa. Settlers from Europe introduced these birds when they went to Australia and New Zealand. The bird's name is derived from the Ancient Greek word *khloris*, which means 'green'.

Greenfinches enjoy a widespread distribution in the UK, feeding on seed, buds, berries and insects, on farmland, woodland and bird tables in towns and gardens. They particularly enjoy black sunflower seeds and birdbaths, sometimes squabbling for the best vantage point. Greenfinches flock with other finches over the winter, searching for food. During the spring, they tend to nest together in small groups in the same bush. As resident birds, they can be seen all year round.

Greenfinches are members of the finch family, Fringillidae, and are a similar size and shape to a house sparrow. They are predominantly olive green, with yellow markings on the wings and tail. Females are duller, with less yellow. Juveniles resemble females but have darker streaks on their body. During the breeding season, male greenfinches put on a display flight, where their olive plumage can be easily recognised with its vibrant flashes of yellow.

Breeding begins in late April or early May, with the nest constructed from twiglets, plant stems and moss, lined with feathers, hair and small roots. Four to six grey/blue eggs with occasional brown speckles are laid. Chicks hatch within two weeks, feeding on regurgitated food from both parents. They fledge in a fortnight. There can be up to three clutches a year, taking the breeding season up until September.

Greenfinches are 15cm long, with a 26cm wingspan and a distinct forked tail. They weigh in the region of 28g and live for two years. The approximately 1,700,000 breeding pairs in the UK are protected by the Wildlife and Countryside Act, 1981. Although numbers fell in the 1970s and 1980s, the 1990s were very good years. More recently, the water-born parasitic disease, trichomonosis, commonly known as bird bath disease, (also affecting pigeons), stops the birds from feeding properly, and has caused a 59% fall in numbers in the last ten years.

Grey Partridge

The grey partridge, *Perdix perdix*, is a popular game bird. It belongs to the pheasant family, Phasianidae. Its Latin name stems from the Ancient Greek legend where the angry Daedalus pushed his nephew Perdix from the sacred hill of Athena. Correspondingly, the grey partridge does not nest in the trees or fly high, generally keeping safely low to the ground, contradicting the line of the Christmas carol.

The grey partridge is found throughout Europe and Asia. This species has been introduced to North America, Australia, New Zealand and South Africa, where it is a popular game bird. In North America, it is termed the Hungarian partridge, or more simply, the Hun.

Whilst once very common, there has been a serious decline in grey partridge numbers in the UK, with an 87% drop from 1970 to 2007, caused by the loss of breeding habitats and food resources. It featured on the UK 'Birds of Conservation Concern' Red List in 2015. There are thought to be 43,000 breeding territories in the UK.

This medium-sized, plump bird measures 30cm long, with a wingspan of 46cm and a weight of around 390g. Both sexes have a striking orange face, white belly and chestnut tail. They have a large, chestnut horseshoe marking on their chest, predominantly in the males, although females can show this too.

The female lays between 10 and 20 olive brown eggs. Sometimes two birds will share a nest, producing up to 40 chicks between them. The grey partridge favours grassland or farmland to breed, in particular cereal crops such as winter wheat. They build their grass nests in hollows in the ground, using the long grass of field margins or the corn itself, for cover. Young birds are a yellow-brown colour. The grey partridge eats seeds, leaves and insects, the latter of which are fed to the young, providing protein for growth, especially within the first 10 days.

The grey partridge does not migrate and will run instead of flying, although it is able to fly low to the ground. Out of the breeding season they will flock in groups of 6 to 15 birds, known as coveys.

There are seven extant subspecies, and the British one, *P.p. perdix*, recognised by Linnaeus in 1758, is found in the UK, and from southern Scandinavia to Italy and the Balkans. The Italian subspecies, *P.p. italica*, has sadly become extinct.

THE SECRET LIFE OF AN ARABLE FIELD

Groundsel

The annual herb, groundsel or *Senecio vulgaris* is also known as 'old man in the spring'. It belongs to the very large, daisy, aster and sunflower family, Asteraceae, and is found across Europe, north Asia and north Africa, and worldwide as a ruderal species. These are plants that are the first to colonise disturbed land, with the word 'ruderal' coming from the Latin, 'rubus', meaning 'rubble'. Groundsel tends to preside over the area for several years, until other native species progressively take over.

Groundsel grows up to 45cm in height. It shares many similarities to *Senecio viscosus*, another herbaceous British annual, but does not have the ray florets or glandular hairs of the latter, which is known as the sticky groundsel. Groundsel itself exhibits hollow, branching stems which are prone to cineraria leaf rust. Soft hairs cover the leaves, which are lobed with saw-toothed edges.

Flowers cluster in groups of 10 to 23. They are small, round and rayless, measuring 6 to 14mm in diameter with black tipped bracts containing the flowers. Ragwort belongs to the same daisy family as groundsel and cross pollination can occur.

Senecio is thought to have come from the Latin word for 'old man' – *senex*. Akin to many members of its family, groundsel will show a fluffy head of seed after it has flowered. These seeds can travel 2 to 3m at winds of 11 to 16km/h, relative to the height of the plant, but this does not explain the enormous distribution the plants have attained. The seeds are tiny, with 1,000 weighing 0.2g, making approximately 2.2 million seeds in a pound. These seeds have an almost complete germination success, although if they are dried and stored, this percentage will drop to 86%. Soil scientists have found that seed emergence does not depend on soil temperature or rainfall.

Groundsel is successful for various reasons, one being that it is frost resistant, another that it is self-pollinating and happy to grow in wastelands and roadsides, as well as agricultural regions and more fertile areas. It is found at up to 500m above sea level. It only emits a shallow taproot, making it easy to establish. Plants develop about 2,000 seeds each, with three generations each year. They travel on the wind, reseeding or attaching to animal fur, allowing them to survive and flourish. Environmental agencies in North America recognise its distribution across all 50 states of the US, all Canadian provinces and northern Mexico, but they are unsure whether to call it native or introduced.

Groundsel is not an especially popular plant for agriculturalists as it hosts a fungus that causes black root rot, affecting alfalfa, peas, carrots, soya beans, chickpeas, cotton, citrus plants, red clover and peanuts. Other funguses and rusts that it is prone to are rust fungus, white rust, sac fungus, groundsel mildew and powdery mildew, among others. Although a primary coloniser, groundsel is not particularly competitive, but it can contaminate crops, particularly as it is fond of disturbed ground.

The plant produces pyrrolizidine alkaloids, which make it attractive to butterflies and moths, such as the larvae of the cinnabar moth, the flame shoulder moth, and ragwort plume moth. Beetles and seed flies, such as the ragwort flea beetle and ragwort seed fly are also hosted, both of which are used for biological control of groundsel in the US and Australia.

Due to these pyrrolizidine alkaloids, groundsel is said to be hepatotoxic to both humans and livestock, causing damage to the liver cells. But it is also noted throughout history as a tonic for the kidneys, a cure for scurvy, epilepsy, laxative and diuretic as well as clearing parasites from the body. Although both the botanists, John Gerard in the sixteenth century, and Nicholas Culpeper in the seventeenth century made use of groundsel, modern research warns against the build-up of these toxic alkaloids.

These alkaloids persist, even if the seeds are dried or they are fermented in silage. Not all animals are affected however. Ruminants, such as sheep and goats are capable of detoxifying the chemicals. Pigs and wild animals are also happy to eat the plant. Cows prefer not to eat it. Horses avoid it too, due to its unpleasant taste, unless the paddock is overgrazed and there are no other plants to eat. Birds feed on the seed freely, without harm.

THE SECRET LIFE OF AN ARABLE FIELD

Hare

Species of hare are indigenous to Africa, Europe and Asia, North America and the Japanese archipelago. Both hares and jackrabbits are members of the genus *Lepus*, belonging to the same family as rabbits. There are 32 species of hare listed worldwide. A jackrabbit is a hare living on the steppes and prairies of North America. Although hares are of comparable size and shape to a rabbit, and share the same herbivorous diet, they differ in several ways. Unlike the rabbit they do not live in groups, rather on their own or in a pair. Their young are capable of looking after themselves soon after birth. A rabbit's young are totally dependent on their mother to begin with. Hares have a shorter gestation period of 30 days, compared to that of a rabbit, which is 42 days. Hares are larger and faster than rabbits, with bigger feet and ears and black markings on their fur. They bolt from predation, whilst rabbits run for cover.

Hares also build what is known as a form, rather than burrowing underground as rabbits do. A form is a nest of grass constructed in a shallow depression above ground. Young are born with their eyes open and fully furred, and so do not need the extra protection that a burrow affords. A group of hares is called a drove, and hares are known as leverets until they reach a year old. Hares possess jointed skulls, often called kinetic skulls, thought to act as a shock absorber whilst running. Although seen in some fish, amphibians, reptiles and birds, as well as dinosaurs, (usually linked to feeding), the hare is unique amongst mammals in having this kind of skull. Other mammals are thought to lack this skull configuration as they need to generate suction in order to suckle.

Hunting for hares and rabbits is not as regulated as it is for other species of game, mainly because they reproduce so quickly and have a wide distribution. During the pioneering days in North America they were frequently eaten, but due to their low-fat content, they are not recommended for survival food.

Several recipes over the years have proved popular. Jugged hare is one of them, where the hare is cut into pieces and marinated with juniper berries and red wine, whilst standing in a tall jug in a pan of water. This is served with the blood of the hare and port. This recipe was mentioned in the eighteenth century book, *The Art of Cookery*, written by Hannah Glasse. She recommends cooking the hare for three hours. Before cooking, the hare is hung by its legs, upside down, allowing the blood to flow to its chest. This blood is then collected, and it can be mixed with red wine vinegar to

stop coagulation. Times have changed. A 2006 survey in the UK revealed that out of 2021 people, only 1.6% of under-25s had heard of jugged hare, whilst 70% would refuse to eat it.

Jews will not eat the meat of a hare (or rabbit) as they do not consider it to be kosher. Muslims are able to eat rabbit, which is halal. Some Muslims will also eat hare, although Shia Muslims avoid it.

Hares are very speedy animals, reaching up to 56km/h. The jackrabbits of North America can cover ground at 64km/h, and are able to jump 3m. Throughout the year the hare is usually a timid creature, but this all changes in spring when they begin to chase one another. This was thought to be a dominant behaviour in boars during the breeding season. The phrase 'mad as a March hare' comes from their 'boxing' behaviour where they are seen punching each other with their front legs, whilst standing on their back legs. Unusually though, this occurs between boars and does, with the females exhibiting this as a way to stop breeding.

THE SECRET LIFE OF AN ARABLE FIELD

Hawthorn

The hawthorn, *Crataegus monogyna*, is native to Europe, northwest Africa and western Asia. It is also known as mayblossom, quickthorn, whitethorn or haw. It has been introduced to other regions of the world and can be considered invasive.

It grows to 5 to 14 metres as a tree but is more commonly cultivated as a shrub. Its dull brown bark contains vertical orange fissures. Thorns decorate the younger branches, being in the region of 12.5mm long. They make this plant especially good for hedging around agricultural fields, with the spines and close branching habit proving useful in containing livestock, particularly when a hedge is laid, which is commonly practiced with hawthorn. At the time of the land enclosures, between the sixteenth and nineteenth centuries, thousands of hawthorn plants were cultivated by landowners to demark their property. In the past decades, these hedges have been ripped up to make way for mechanised farming, and the effective spines of the hawthorn have been exchanged for electric fences or barbed wire.

Hawthorn leaves are in the region of 20 to 40 mm long and are obovate and lobed. The flowers are about 10mm wide, and show in late spring, from May to the beginning of June. They are hermaphrodite, exhibiting both male and female characteristics and they grow in corymbs or clusters of 5 to 25 blooms. These flowers provide food for, and are indeed pollinated by, bees, wasps and other insects. The fruit produced later in the year are small, dark red and oval, about 10mm long, looking like a berry, but are actually a pome in that they hold a seed, like a pear or apple. Birds, such as the thrush and waxwing, eat these haws in the winter, spreading the seeds as a waste product.

The haws can be eaten by humans, and are used in the kitchen to make jams, jellies, syrups and wine. They can also be added to brandy to improve the taste. Petals are sprinkled on salads in spring. An ancient recipe from around 1390 was written down by the Master Chef to King Richard II in a document called *The Frome of Cury*, where he describes adding hawthorn petals to spinee, a stew made with almond milk.

Famous hawthorns include the Glastonbury or Holy Thorn, which legend recounts was propagated by Joseph of Arimathea when he brought Christianity to Britain in the first century AD. He was the owner of the tomb in which Jesus was placed after the crucifixion. Joseph thrust his hawthorn staff into the ground whilst visiting Glastonbury and it was said to take root, and henceforth grow into a tree. This tree was remarkable in that it flowered twice a year, both in spring and at Christmas,

subsequently being known as the variety 'biflora'. A custom, whereby a flowering branch is sent to the British monarch every year at Christmas, was inaugurated by James Montague, Bishop of Bath and Wells during the reign of James I. The Glastonbury tree survived up until the 1640s, when it was cut down during the English Civil War by the Roundheads, as they considered it superstitious. A replacement was planted at Wearyall Hill in 1951, but vandals again cut the branches off in 2010.

Another ancient hawthorn tree can be found in the churchyard of the village of Hethel, in Norfolk. Known as the Hethel Old Thorn, it is said to be over 700 years old, cultivated in the thirteenth century.

Hawthorn wood burns well with a good heat and small amount of smoke.

Hazel Dormouse

The hazel dormouse, *Muscardinus avellanarius*, is native to northern parts of Europe and Asia Minor. It is the only dormouse present in the UK, although the edible dormouse, *Glis glis*, has recently been introduced by accident, escaping from Lord Rothschild's estate in Hertfordshire, and subsequently becoming established. Although not native, the hazel dormouse found its way to Ireland, first seen in 2010 enjoying the hedgerows of Co. Kildare. Numbers are reducing in the UK, by a third since 2000. This is due to loss of their woodland habitat and changes in farm management, with possibly implications from a changed climate too. Although hazel dormice enjoy hedgerow and scrub, they are most at home in deciduous woodland.

The hazel dormouse is 10cm long, with a 6cm tail. It weighs around 20g, although this doubles before hibernation. Fur is on the orange/reddish/brown spectrum, with a lighter belly. They possess large, black eyes, small ears and hairy tails.

The dormouse is active at night, traversing tree branches in search of food. Hibernation is from October to early May. They spend the winter nesting at ground level, amongst hazel stools, leaves or wood stacks, which give a reasonably constant level of humidity and heat. In spring, when the dormouse awakes, they build a nest from leaves and grasses deep in the shrubbery. If the weather is adverse or there are not enough food supplies, it will enter a sleeping state, or 'torpor', to conserve energy.

Dormice are noted for opening a hazelnut with a small, circular hole. Other rodents, such as the bank vole, also adopt this manner, whilst squirrels and birds will break the shell or create an erratically shaped hole. Hazelnuts are the favoured food for dormice to put weight on for winter. Squirrels compete for the same food resources.

The dormouse eats above ground level, within the safety of branches, protecting it from predators such as the badger, fox, weasel and stoat, and also pet cats. Footsteps and hooves of humans and deer pose another danger, as they would crush the dormice without too much thought. Other hazards are farming operations, such as aggressive hedge-trimming. The hazel dormouse, (and the edible dormouse), are protected under the Wildlife and Countryside Act in the UK 1981, due to their woodland and hedgerow habitat being destroyed.

Food sources are many and varied across the year, with hazel being the main ingredient. If hazel is in short supply, the dormouse will turn to the fruit of hornbeam and blackthorn, with the berries of alder buckthorn also providing fat resources before hibernation. The insect population, particularly aphids and butterfly larva are enjoyed, and the dormice will also eat the flowers from oak, honeysuckle, bramble, hawthorn, sycamore, the wayfaring tree, broom and sweet chestnut. Acorns are disregarded, but the dormice will eat the fruit of honeysuckle, bramble, blackthorn (sloe berries), wayfaring tree and the otherwise poisonous yew. Immature seeds from willow and ash, hornbeam and birch seeds are all eagerly consumed.

Honeysuckle bark is used for nest building. Brambles are favoured nest spots, as their thorns provide a great deal of safety.

THE SECRET LIFE OF AN ARABLE FIELD

Hedgehog

The hedgehog belongs to the family Erinaceidae. There are 17 species of hedgehog in all, and they are found throughout Europe, Asia and Africa, with introductions to New Zealand. The hedgehog native to North America has become extinct, so now the Americas are hedgehog-less, as is Australia.

Hedgehogs are related distantly to shrews and date back 15 million years. They are not related to spiny anteaters or porcupines, the latter of which are rodents.

Hedgehogs were named in 1450, using the Middle English 'heyghoge' meaning 'hedge', where they tend to live, and 'hoge' describing their snout, which looks like a pig's.

The spines are easily the most recognisable feature of a hedgehog. These spines are hollow and made of keratin. Hedgehogs differ from porcupines in that their spines are not poisonous or barbed, and they do not fall out. Quilling does occur in young hedgehogs as they lose their baby spines, which are replaced with adult quills. Hedgehogs are brown, with spines having lighter ends. Blonde hedgehogs can be found on the island of Alderney.

The hedgehog's main defensive strategy is to roll up once threatened, protecting the soft underbelly, face and feet, and presenting a quilled ball to the attacker. It has two large muscles on its back which controls the movement of its spines. Birds, such as owls, as well as ferrets, foxes and badgers are all predator species. The badger and the hedgehog compete for food, and areas with a large badger population are shown to support very few hedgehogs, so much so that hedgehog rescue centres will not release hedgehogs into badger dense areas.

The hedgehog is most active at night. They spend most of the day snoozing under bushes, grasses or rocks, or in self-made dens underground. They spend the winter in hibernation, but if the weather is mild and food is available, the length of this period will be shortened or given up altogether. During hibernation, the hedgehog's body temperature falls to 2°C, rising back to 30 to 35°C when it wakes up.

A hedgehog is quite vocal, and will make a series of grunts, squeals and snuffles. They exhibit behaviour called 'anointing', whereby on discovering a new scent, it will be licked and ingested into the mouth, with a froth created. The hedgehog will cover their spines with this froth. Some say this is a useful camouflage tool, acting as a defence against predation. Some birds also show this characteristic, in a process called 'anting', whereby they rub insects onto their feathers and skin or wallow in a pool of ants. Why, is not exactly yet clear!

Hedgehogs developed independently, as did pigs, honey badgers and mongooses, to have a mutation in their nicotinic acetylcholine receptor that inhibits the snake venom α-neurotoxin from taking effect. They are therefore protected from venomous snake bites.

They are omnivorous, eating a range of foods, such as snails, insects, frogs, snakes, birds' eggs and carrion, as well as a more vegetarian diet of grass roots, berries, mushrooms and even melons.

Three to seven young are produced after a gestation period of 35 to 58 days. The young are blind at birth. In order to protect the mother during birthing, their quills remain below the surface of the skin, and will begin to emerge a few hours after birth. The father may take it upon himself to destroy any male hedgehogs in the litter. Hedgehogs can live for up to seven years in the wild, and substantially more in captivity.

Hedgehogs can be kept as pets in Europe, but this is illegal in Scandinavia as well as some US states. The Italian government stipulates that wild hedgehogs are not to be kept as pets. The usual hedgehog pet is a hybrid of the white-bellied hedgehog and

THE SECRET LIFE OF AN ARABLE FIELD

the North African hedgehog, but other species, such as the long-eared and Indian long-eared, are also popular.

The trouble with introduced animals is that they tend not to have any predators. New Zealand found that the hedgehog killed a large variety of native species, such as ground-nesting birds and lizards. Scottish islands faced a similar dilemma, with bird colonies on North Uist and Benbecula in the Outer Hebrides being particularly hard hit. Tempers rose in 2003 when nearly 700 hedgehogs were killed in this region. Animal welfare groups got involved. They had their way, and by 2007, it was illegal to kill a hedgehog. Elimination continued in the following year, but this time hedgehogs were trapped and transported for life on the mainland.

Hedgehog casualties on the roads are common. Males are hardest hit in May and June, whilst female deaths peak in June, July and August. The former is probably due to activity around the breeding season, and the latter a result of the subsequent independence of the young.

Hedgehogs have been eaten since Ancient Egyptian times, as well as more recently in the Late Middle Ages. They are also sought after throughout Europe, Asia and Africa for use in traditional medicine and even witchcraft. The Bedouins use hedgehog meat to cure arthritis and rheumatism. Moroccans burn the skin and quills to help with fevers, impotence and bladder disorders, using the blood to treat ringworm and warts. Romani people still eat hedgehogs, either boiling or roasting them.

Herb Robert

Herb Robert, *Geranium robertianum*, is found in shady areas of grassland, woodland, hedgerows and coastal habitats. It grows up to 30cm and can be seen from May to September. It is a species of cranesbill, indigenous to Europe, regions of Asia, North America and north Africa.

Its pretty pink, five-petalled flowers, 8 to 15mm wide, are held on erect, reddish stems. Foliage is deeply divided and will also turn red towards the end of its season.

It has been used medicinally for centuries, to stop diarrhoea and soothe liver and gallbladder issues. It also helps toothache and nosebleeds, and has the ability to heal wounds. It is said that its crushed leaves act as an insect repellent. More recently, scientists have confirmed the antioxidant, antimicrobial, anti-inflammatory, anti-hyperglycaemic and cytotoxic properties of herb Robert. These are due to the high levels of phenolic compounds in the plant, which also contains tannins and geraniin.

Holly Blue Butterfly

The holly blue butterfly, *Celastrina argiolus*, can be found across Europe, north Africa and into Asia. There has been a population increase in the UK of around 40% since the 1970s. They favour woodland habitats, but are also common in gardens, parks, hedgerows and churchyards, laying eggs in holly in the spring and ivy in late summer. They can be differentiated from other blue butterflies as they are seen earlier in spring, and fly up to tree tops and tall shrubs, whereas other blues tend to fly nearer ground level.

Both males and females have blue underwings. The males' wings are brighter, with a narrow black margin, whereas the females' wings are paler with a larger, browner, margin. Both genders have small black spots on their underwings, in contrast to the common blue butterfly.

They are small butterflies, belonging to the Lycaenidae, or gossamer-winged family. They have a wingspan of 35mm. In addition to holly and ivy, caterpillars feed on spindle, dogwood, snowberries, gorses and bramble.

Holly

There are around 480 species of holly in the *Ilex* genus, part of the family Aquifoliaceae. They are found throughout the world, with huge variation, from evergreen to deciduous, trees to climbers, in both temperate and tropical parts of the planet.

Holly is thought to have been around for over 82 million years. It prospered in the laurel forests common to the Neogene period, 20 million years ago. The more drought tolerant *Ilex aquifolium* evolved when the Mediterranean Basin dried up and mountains were formed during the Pliocene period 5 million years ago. Laurel forests retreated as a result of a less moist environment. The temperate broadleaf evergreen landscape characterised by these laurels came to an end during the Pleistocene period or Ice Age, 12,500 years ago. When this happened, many hollies became extinct as they could not cope with the changing conditions.

The species that we know and love is the evergreen *Ilex aquifolium*, which is the European or English holly. Widespread throughout the western and southern parts of the Continent, it can also be found in the northwest of Africa and southwest Asia. It is one of only a few native evergreen trees found in the UK, growing to heights of 10 to 25 metres, living to 500 years, but more commonly to 100. Its four-lobed white flowers are pollinated by bees. There are separate male and female plants, although it takes 4 to 12 years, when the plants start flowering, to determine its gender.

They can grow in a dense thicket; often, they will be found in an oak or beech wood. The English holly is a non-native, invasive species on the west coast of North America, enjoying the shade and crowding out the native plants. Holly is a pioneer species.

Holly berries are actually drupes or stone fruit. Throughout the world, they are found in different colours, ranging from yellow to green, red to black. English holly berries are vivid red. Holly seeds go through a lengthy dormancy period, with difficult germination requirements which can take up to three years to break.

The berries of *Ilex aquifolium* can cause diarrhoea and vomiting. Holly leaves also create these problems. If more than 20 berries are eaten by a child, it can result in death. Domestic animals and pets are also susceptible to the caffeine and theobromine. It is thought the ilicin causes vomiting. English holly contains some powerful chemicals, such as chlorogenic acid, caffeoylshikimic acid, caffeic acid, caffeoyl derivatives, feruloylquinic acid, quercetin, quinic acid,

THE SECRET LIFE OF AN ARABLE FIELD

kaempferol, saponins, tannins, rutin, caffeine, theobromine and the yellow pigment, ilexanthin.

That being said, Paraguayan tea is made from yerba mate or *Ilex paraguariensis*, with other teas cultivated from *I. kaushue* (Kuding tea) and the aptly named *I. vomitoria* (Yaupon tea). Traditional medicine makes use of holly as a diuretic, a laxative and for soothing fever.

In the past, before the use of turnips, *Ilex aquifolium* was eaten during the winter by cattle and sheep. The holly was taken from the upper branches of the tree, where it is less spiny.

Holly has also found its way into the garden, being represented by hybrids and cultivars such as Highclere holly, which is *Ilex x altaclerensis* (*I. aquifolium x I. perado*) and the blue holly, which is *Ilex x meserveae* (*I. aquifolium x I. rugosa*). The Royal Horticultural Society has awarded their Award of Garden Merit to the following cultivars: of *Ilex x altaclerensis*: 'Belgica Aurea', 'Camelliifolia', 'Golden King' and 'Lawsoniana'. Hollies are good for hedging and they are easy to shape with pruning.

Holly is well known and loved at Christmas time, where it has provided symbolism since Medieval days, being used in wreaths and decorations. The carol *The Holly and the Ivy* is said to represent Jesus' crown of thorns, with the ivy denoting the Virgin Mary. Holly was used by the Romans to celebrate the ancient festival of Saturnalia, the December celebration of Saturn and the precursor of Christmas.

Holly, a white wood, was traditionally used for making bagpipes before tropical woods such as ebony, crocus wood and African blackwood came into fashion.

Holly berries provide a feast for birds and wild animals during the winter. In October and November, the berries have a high ilicin content, making them very bitter. They soften after they have been through several frosts, so that by mid-winter they are a delicious treat for birds and rodents. The bushes also provide protection for birds from storms and predators, as the spiny leaves of the holly make an impassable barrier. A mass of holly can provide refuge for a deer.

The insignificant holly flowers are eaten by the larvae of the double-striped pug moth (*Gymnoscelis rufifasciata*). Other insects include the moths *Bucculatrix ilecella*, which feeds exclusively on holly, and *Ectropis crepuscularia*.

Honeybee

The honeybee is found throughout the world in all continents except Antarctica. Part of the genus *Apis*, (meaning 'bee' in Latin), they are recognised by their large colonies, wax nests and stockpiling of honey, which attracts predators such as honey badgers, bears and humans. At the beginning of this century, seven species of honeybee were recorded, with 44 subspecies. The most common species is the western honeybee, *Apis mellifera*, which translates as 'honey-bearing bee'.

All honeybees are eusocial, which means they have a high level of social organisation, with a lone female giving birth to the young and non-reproductive individuals helping care for them. The colony is made up of the queen and many female workers who seldom breed, as well as male drones, whose role it is to mate with the queen. Each colony can be made up of tens of thousands of individuals. Communication is sophisticated, using both pheromones and dance.

The western honeybee was one of the first insects to be farmed by humans, both for the honey and its pollination abilities. The vast range of the honeybee, covering most of the world, makes it an incredibly vital tool for agriculture. It has suffered from diseases and pests, such as colony collapse disorder and the *Varroa* mite. From 2019 it has been recorded by the IUCN on their Red List as critically endangered, due to serious falls in numbers.

The western honeybee spread from Asia, throughout Africa, Europe and the Middle East. It was imported to North America in the early 1600s, and later to South America, Australia, New Zealand and the east of Asia.

Western honeybees have shown considerable adaptations to the environment as they have spread across the globe. They link in to the life cycle of local plants and change their colony habits accordingly. In colder regions, when the temperature falls below 10°C the bees cluster in a ball inside their nest, which keeps them warm. They have also evolved their feeding behaviour to suit desert conditions. In doing so, they have created 28 subspecies, which can still reproduce with others within the same species.

The western honeybee population breed whilst swarming. This takes place, in most areas, during the spring and summer, when there are plenty of flowers in bloom, offering pollen and nectar. The colony's queen gives birth to 12 to 24 new queens, developing from an embryo, into larva and thence to pupa. At this stage the old queen and about 60% of her workers will fly to a new location to build a colony. The newly adult daughter-queens will fight each other to the death until only one is victorious.

The new queen will then lay her eggs. She can produce offspring without fertilisation, similar to other bees, wasps and ants. These will be male, but to lay female eggs they must be fertilised. To do this, she goes on a few nuptial flights, where she mates with up to 20 drones (males), returning to the colony to lay her eggs. This whole process takes about 14 days from her first emerging from the pupa stage.

Nectar is transformed by the female worker bees, which make up about 90% of the colony. They remove the water content in the nectar (80 to 95%) by evaporation, fanning their wings and generating heat. This reduces the risk of mould, and in the process they create honey. They cover this with wax, and it can be stored for a considerable length of time. In the UK, western honeybees hibernate over winter, at which point the queen refrains from her egg-laying duties. Bees eat some of the honey that they have stored. It is thought that the increased day-lengths from 21 December onwards starts the queen laying again.

The four life stages of a western honeybee are egg, larvae, pupa and adult; a process called complete metamorphosis. These stages can occur concurrently throughout the year. Each honeycomb cell will house a single egg, laid by the queen. The larva stage lasts around seven days, during which the emerging bee lacks eyes and legs. It is fed by 'nurse' bees, which are a variant of the worker bees. They fasten it in its cell, so that it can begin to pupate. A further seven days goes by, at which point they emerge as adults. These nursing cells are usually all grouped together, whilst other areas are used for pollen and honey.

THE SECRET LIFE OF AN ARABLE FIELD

These new western honeybees are born into a regimented structure. They spend the first 10 days of their adult life cleaning the colony and giving food to new larvae. Then they move on to helping construct cells, and on days 17 to 20, they learn how to store nectar and pollen given by more advanced workers. After learning these duties, the bee will be allowed the freedom to forage; a role that carries on indefinitely.

Female worker bees cannot reproduce, but if they undergo extreme stress, some subspecies do lay. Since they lack certain reproductive organs, these eggs will hatch into male drones. Females have an ovipositor, like the queen, which the males lack. It is only the females, therefore, which can sting. This 'stinger' is also used to lay eggs. The female's ovipositor is barbed, unlike the queens. These barbs attach to the skin. They contain a venom sac, which lodges in the skin. A female worker will die after stinging a human or animal as its barb will get stuck in the skin, unlike that of the queen, who survives.

A western honeybee queen will live approximately three to five years. Towards the end of her life, her offspring will tend to be male. The resultant lack of female workers means beekeepers usually start with a new queen every year or two. A worker's lifespan in temperate regions, such as the UK, is determined by the length of winter. Bees born in the spring and summer will live less than a month. The eggs laid in autumn will survive the cold weather due to clustering. Mortality at all times of the year is high, with 1% of the community dying daily. Apart from the queen, there will be a total turnover in population every four months.

The queen is considerably larger than the female workers, and has a mature, fully working reproductive system. During the first three days, all newly laid eggs are nourished by royal jelly, which is rich in protein. An emerging queen will stay on her royal jelly diet after that, whilst the other eggs are fed field-gathered flower pollen, known as 'bee bread'. The queen's diet allows her reproductive system to mature, which is vital given that she will give birth to an entire colony.

When the queen is reaching the end of her useful life, there is a change in her pheromones, which is sensed throughout the hive. These pheromones control the worker bees, but a decline in their potency usually leads to the death of the queen at the hands of her workers. Another reason for a new queen is the sudden death of the old queen. The worker bees will then try to bring on a new queen from either eggs or larvae, by continuing their diet of royal jelly.

Once the new queen is born, she will take a few days to find her way around the hive before flying to a meeting place, generally around 10m from ground level. There she will find drones, not just from her colony, but nearby colonies too. They pick up her scent from her pheromones and mate with her in the air. Female workers can also take advantage of this meeting, by emitting the same scent as the queen and thereby mating with the drones. The queen mates numerous times, often over several days, until she is full of egg-laying potential. The queen will inseminate her female eggs using the reserves of sperm that she has accumulated through mating. The male drone cells are larger and are not fertilised.

The weather and therefore, food availability, will determine how many eggs are actually laid, and how quickly. Egg-laying is reduced in autumn and can stop completely in winter. The queen lays more than 2,500 eggs a day at her peak, which weigh more than she does. In a well-run colony, only the queen will lay the eggs.

Female workers are busy around the nest, raising and feeding the young and creating the social organisation of the hive. By contrast the male drone's purpose is to mate with the queen. Males do not hunt for pollen or nectar. Having mated, they die at once. Fertilising the queen creates a deadly convulsive response. Drones can sometimes be banished from the nest before winter. They will not survive the cold, and since they do not feed themselves, they can also die of food deprivation. They are about 1.5 times larger than female workers, and their presence in the colony can be useful for temperature control. They usually centre themselves in the middle of the hive, presumably because their sperm is more viable at warmer temperatures, although they cease to be effective at temperatures lower than 25°C.

A female worker can give birth to a drone, but this causes considerable conflict within the organisation of the hive. 'Worker policing' occurs, where other workers will seek to remove these eggs, showing hostility towards the reproductive worker. They determine these eggs using pheromones. If the queen dies, more female workers will take the pains to lay eggs, producing a generation of drones before the colony collapses.

A temperature of 35°C is ideal in the nest for making beeswax and for the growth of the young. It can fall in winter to 20°C. The ideal air temperature for foraging is 22°C as heat collected in the flight muscles can disperse. If temperatures are higher than this, the honeybee produces a drop of liquid, called a 'honey crop droplet', which cools its body by around 10°C. If the honeybee wants to fly in cool conditions, it will shiver, to warm up its muscles, stopping during flight to continue to do so if necessary. The temperature range at which a western honeybee can fly varies from 7°C to 50°C, although foraging decreases beyond 38°C.

Early evidence of human interaction with bees goes back to 7,000bc, seen in rock art in Spain and France showing humans gathering honey. Honeybees were domesticated very early on. In ancient Egypt, workers are depicted on the walls of the sun temple blowing smoke into hives from which they are removing honeycombs, dating back to the Fifth Dynasty in 2400bc.

A beekeeper can buy a mated queen and a number of workers or an entire colony. This originated in 1622, when the state of Virginia in the US purchased bee colonies from England. It was not until the latter part of the 1880s when modern methods of queen production and the dividing and creating of colonies were first practiced.

Contemporary hives are capable of being moved, so the beekeeper can place them near crops that need pollination. There is much money to be made in this service, as wild pollinators have decreased in number. The almond crops in California require pollination in February, which is too early in the year for the vast bee numbers. Over a third of all honeybees in the US are used in this pollination event, with one hive employed for every acre. Bees are also transported to New York and Washington for apple pollination. Western honeybees were valued at creating $200 billion in 2005, across the globe, through the pollination of crops.

The honey that the bees produce contains sugars such as glucose and fructose, with anti-fungal and anti-bacterial properties. Honey does not degrade over time, instead crystallising. Beeswax, created by glands in the bee's stomach, is harvested by humans for candles and wax seals. Bee bread, another by-product, is formed from pollen. Humans eat this, although it can cause an allergic reaction in some. Bee brood, which is the collective term for the eggs, larvae and pupae of the western honeybee is eaten in some cultures, containing similar quantities of protein as beef or chicken. Royal jelly is believed to help rheumatoid arthritis and boosts the immune system.

Western honeybees are finding it hard to survive in today's world. In the UK, the Varroa mite struck in the 1990s. This mite can only reproduce within a honeybee nest, clinging on to the bee and sucking its fat, causing a genetic RNA virus and deformed wing virus, ultimately leading to the death of the colony. It is a major cause of the worldwide fall in bee numbers. The mid-2000s saw a surge of colony collapse disorder in the US, in both wild and domesticated populations. It is known that pesticides are creating many problems for honeybees with increased resistance of some bee pests also a factor.

The western honeybee faces predation from several wasps in the UK, including the Asian giant hornet – the world's largest hornet, as well as robber flies – otherwise known as assassin flies due to their aggressive behaviour to their insect prey. Some praying mantises, pond skaters, the European beewolf, and dragonflies such as green darner dragonfly, also eat the western honeybee.

Western honeybees are also prone to attack from various spiders such as raft spiders found in the UK and Europe, and lynx spiders, which generally hunt on plants without building a nest. Frogs also enjoy a tasty snack of honeybee, and across the world, birds such as the bee-eater, hummingbird, and tyrant flycatchers also feast on the bees. The summer tanager, a bird native to the US, will wait on a branch near the colony and catch a multitude of bees in one go. Mammals, such as bears, racoons, badgers, skunks and shrews, all prey on the bees and their honey.

Honeysuckle

There are two honeysuckles native to Britain. One is the common honeysuckle, *Lonicera periclymenum*, and the other is *L. xylosteum*. The latter is known as the fly honeysuckle, or fly woodbine, and it is a deciduous shrub which produces red, seldom yellow, berries which cause stomach pain and vomiting if more than around 20 are eaten.

L. periclymenum is found throughout Europe, north Africa, Turkey and the Caucasus. It is seen at northern latitudes up to the south of Norway and Sweden. It is part of the Caprifoliaceae family and can grow over 7 metres in height, vigorously climbing in woodland, hedgerows and scrub.

Flowers are tubular, with two lips, creamy yellow with pinkish/red exteriors. The smell they emit is strong, being much more powerful at night, when it can be perceived over 400 metres away. Night-flying moths, such as the hummingbird hawk-moth are pollinators as well as long-tongue bees.

Autumn berries are food for birds, such as warblers, bullfinches and thrushes. Mice are known to make their nests from the bark, and are among other small animals feeding on the flowers, enjoying the sweet, high-energy nectar.

Honeysuckle has found favour in the garden, due to its dense climbing habit, and many cultivars have been developed.

The plant does suffer from the honeysuckle leaf miner, *Chromatomyia aprilina*.

Hops

The twining stems of the hop, *Humulus lupulus*, can be found climbing in hedgerows and woodland edges in the UK, flowering between July and September. The leaves are deeply divided, possessing three to five lobes, and are placed opposite one another. They have a rough texture, with serrated margins. Flowers are a greenish-yellow, with males and females being situated on different plants. Females form catkins. These cone-shaped fruit ripen from green to brown. They have the characteristic aroma of garlic, apples and yeast, and contain oils such as lupulin and oleoresin. The latter of these is what gives beer its individual flavour. The bitter taste of beer comes from iso-alpha acids present in the fruit.

White bryony is another climbing plant that bears a resemblance to hops, although its leaves are situated alternately, and its fruit are red and poisonous.

The hop is useful to wildlife, as it provides a secure retreat for birds and insects within its branches, and insects enjoy its nectar source.

The flowering stalks of hop have been utilised in the UK in brewing since at least the Middle Ages, due to their ability to stop bacteria from multiplying – the technical term

being 'bacteriostatic'. As well as preserving the beer, they create foaming and certain aromas, such as fruity or citrus flavours. Hops help anxiety and insomnia, and can be used as a sedative for animals and humans; for example, by filling a pillow full of hops.

Before hops were utilised, beer was made with 'gruit'; a blend of herbs and flowers, such as dandelion, marigold, ground ivy and heather. The first recorded cultivation of hops is said to be 736AD in Germany, but it was not until the thirteenth century that hops in beer-making began to take precedence over gruit. The British first tasted hop beer when it was imported from the Netherlands in 1400, but it took until 1524, when Henry VIII was on the throne, before hops were grown in Kent, as it was previously considered a 'wicked and pernicious weed'.

Hops grow best in moist, temperate climates, thriving in similar soils to potatoes. The top hop producing country in 2017 was the US with 44,325 tons, followed by Germany with 39,000 tons. The UK produced 1,400 tons in that year.

The hop industry does not require pollinated seeds, therefore only female plants are grown, which are propagated vegetatively. If grown from seed, male plants will be thrown away.

Hops can be used to make herbal teas and soft drinks. New growth on the vine is edible and can be prepared like asparagus. Research into HRT is looking into the use of hops, as well as for menstrual ailments. Dermatitis can occasionally occur from handling hops. The plant is toxic to dogs.

THE SECRET LIFE OF AN ARABLE FIELD

Horse Chestnut

The horse chestnut, *Aesculus hippocastanum*, belongs to the soapberry family, Sapindaceae, which also includes the maple, lychee and ackee. It is a deciduous tree, reaching 39 metres in height and is synoecious, having male and female organs in the same flower. It is known for its distinctive seed: the conker. It is a fast-growing tree, thriving on most soils, although it does need a lot of space.

The crown of the tree is bell-shaped, with pendulous outer branches. Palmate leaves are large: 60cm in diameter, made up of five to seven leaflets arranged oppositely, emanating from a single, central point. When the leaves fall, they leave a scar on the bark which has a horseshoe shape, as well as the seven 'nails' used by the farrier when shoeing a horse.

Flowers grow in panicles, i.e. a cluster of flowers growing at the end of a branch or shoot. These stand 10 to 30cm tall and each panicle contains 20 to 50 flowers. They are white with a yellow/pink marking on the bottom of the petals.

Around one to five fruits will develop on each panicle, with a green, prickly casing holding one or occasionally two to three seeds or nuts, known as conkers. They are called 'buckeyes' in the US as they resemble the eyes of a deer. Glossy-brown conkers are 2 to 4cm wide, with a white scar at their base.

The red or pink horse chestnut present in the UK is *Aesculus x carnea*, a hybrid between the horse chestnut and the red buckeye, (*Aesculus pavia*), from North America. It has darker leaves in comparison to the horse chestnut and is usually smaller.

The Turks used to use the conkers to treat horses which were panting and coughing from the respiratory disorder known as broken wind or recurrent airway obstruction, similar to COPD in humans. This has to be done with care, as conkers can cause trembling and dizziness in horses if ingested.

The tree is thought to have been introduced to the UK from the Balkans in the late sixteenth century. It grows well in temperate regions, be it in New Zealand or the UK, where the horse chestnut has been grown in decorative avenues from as early as the seventeenth century. Trees can be found as far north as Norway, Iceland and the bee-keeping Canadian province of Alberta where it thrives in the cooler summers.

Conkers has been a game played by children for centuries. The name comes from the word 'conqueror'. Initially children used cobnuts or snail shells, and it was not until the eighteenth century that horse chestnuts became popular. In the German state of Bavaria, before fridges were invented, horse chestnut trees were grown to cool the beer, which was stored underground in caverns. The huge canopies and shallow

roots of the tree, that would not disturb the cellars, made it a popular choice, leading to the development of the beer garden in the nineteenth century.

In both the First and Second World Wars the British Government requested supplies of conkers from the British people. The starch that they contained was used to make ammunition. Although starch could be found from other sources, the government particularly asked for conkers to avoid using valuable food supplies.

Conkers are known to be poisonous, due to their alkaloid, saponin and glucoside content. The 20% level of esculin that can be extracted from the conker has been tested for its vascular protection and anti-inflammatory properties. However, the conker, leaf, flower and bark of the horse chestnut are toxic and should not be eaten. The Food and Drug Administration in the USA has classified the conker as an unsafe herb.

The tree itself is prone to bleeding canker, which was first reported in the 1970s in the UK, although much earlier, (in the 1930s), in the US. Around 50% of all horse chestnuts are now affected in Britain, and the disease is found throughout Western Europe. Bacteria spreads by wind-blown rainfall and infects the trunk and larger branches of the tree, until the water supply to the crown is cut off, and the tree eventually dies.

Horse chestnut wood has limited economic value. It is a pale cream/brown, light and weak. It is absorbent, and therefore good for making containers to store fruit. It is also used for children's toys, and until recently, artificial limbs.

THE SECRET LIFE OF AN ARABLE FIELD

Ivy

English ivy or *Hedera helix*, is a species of evergreen plant, native to the majority of Europe and the west of Asia. It belongs to the family Araliaceae, which contains 12 to 15 other species of Hedera. The specific epithet, *helix*, was first used in the sixteenth century, finding its roots in the Latin word for spiral shaped.

Ivy grows 20 to 30m, covering trees, cliffs or walls. It has aerial rootlets which form along the length of the stem. These adventitious roots contain tiny hairs which grow and push into miniscule cracks, sending out adhesive nanoparticles which become rigid and woody as lignin is deposited by the cell walls. This dries out and thereby the ivy manages to cling to the façade.

Ivy can also grow as groundcover if there is nothing available to climb.

Hedera helix flourishes in deeply shaded environments with a neutral pH. Direct sunlight can cause it to dry out over winter. Its leaves are arranged alternately, and they are 5 to 10cm in length, with a petiole of 1.5 to 2cm. Juvenile leaves have five lobes emanating from a single point, and their stems will be climbing. Adult leaves are cordate – heart-shaped – and they will be the ones that flower, high up in the crowns of trees.

Flowers are very important for bees and other insects, with over 70 species feeding and pollinating them as they move from flower to flower. They are produced from the end of summer to the end of autumn and are flush with nectar, when not many other sources are around. These green/yellow flowers are 3 to 5cm wide and arranged in umbels.

Fruit is in the form of dark berries, 6 to 8mm wide, and again, since they don't ripen until well into the winter, they are an invaluable food source for more than 16 species of bird. Humans eating them may feel rather unwell. Each berry is composed of one to five seeds, which will be dispersed in the bird's droppings. The thick haven provided by the leaves creates a sanctuary for a wide variety of wildlife.

Ivy can withstand temperatures of -23.3°C.

Ivy is a popular horticultural choice, due to its fast-growing nature. It can be used on buildings to provide insulation in the winter, as well as a cooling effect in the summer. It also has benefits in preventing too much soil moisture around the house. If removed, it will leave distinguishing marks on the walls. Over 30 cultivars have been developed, showing a range of features, such as variegated or yellow leaves, purple stems or dwarf growth. However, English ivy is treated as an invasive species in much

of the US, southern Australia and New Zealand with its sale or import banned in some areas. If allowed to grow freely it will smother all other vegetation, including trees. To remove it, ivy has to be cut of at the base of its trunk, and the roots dug up or killed.

Ivy nowadays is used in cough medicine. Its leaves and berries have a history in curing bronchitis and other throat ailments. Leaves can cause an allergic reaction in some people, probably as a result of the falcarinol present, which can also be found in carrots. The British herbalist, John Gerald, prescribed the use of ivy leaves soaked in water for eye treatments in 1597.

THE SECRET LIFE OF AN ARABLE FIELD

Jackdaw

The western jackdaw, *Corvus monedula*, belongs to the crow family. It is native to Europe, north Africa and the west of Asia. Northern and eastern populations in this range will migrate south in the colder months. There are four subspecies of the bird, identified by their head feathers.

Numbers in the UK are up, with data from 1970 to 2007 showing a 136% increase. It is thought that 15.5 to 45 million jackdaws inhabit Europe alone, with a global territory of 1 to 10 million square kilometres.

The birds are approximately 35cm from head to tail. Feathers are black, with a purple sheen. They have a grey neck and light silver/grey eyes. Both males and females look the same. They moult every year between June and September.

Jackdaws inhabit farmland, woodland, and cliffs, and are also found in towns and cities. They are known to be intelligent, exhibiting tool use. The birds have a strong social structure, constructing stick nests in trees or buildings. They mate for life, becoming sexually mature in their second year. The female lays four to five light blue/green eggs in each clutch, covered in brown flecks.

Carl Linnaeus first chronicled the jackdaw in the eighteenth century, choosing its specific name from the Latin stem for 'money' as the bird showed a fondness for picking up coins. The common name for the bird was in use from the sixteenth century, with 'jack' meaning 'small'. Before that, the birds were simply called 'daw', coming from the Old English word 'dawe'. They have also been known as 'the chimney-sweep bird', due to their nesting habits, or 'sea crow'. A flock of jackdaws is called a 'clattering', or alternatively a 'train'.

Their flight vocalisation is metallic and squeaky, used to welcome others. They have a different call when feeding. A chick will manage a small cheep to begin with, and gain its adult voice after 20 days. They have an alarm call used to taunt predators, for example the least weasel, and larger birds, such as the magpie or raven. Flocks of jackdaws will converse in their roosts before going to sleep at night. Roosts of over 40,000 birds have been seen in Europe; a larger colony of birds makes it harder for a predator to raid. Like a parrot, the jackdaw can learn to copy the human voice. The jackdaw, similar to the magpie, shows an interest in gleaming materials, such as jewellery.

There is a strong social hierarchy in the jackdaw world. An unmated female is the lowest in the pecking order, getting the least access to food and shelter. Young males establish their status before choosing a mate, who will then occupy the same

ranking as her partner. The flock generally accept the *status quo*, but will reinforce the hierarchy if need be, with aggression and threatening behaviour, watched by other members of the flock, who vocalise their support. Occasionally, if a pair cannot reproduce, they may separate, but if they stick together for more than six months, they will stay together for life. If one partner dies, the survivor may be expelled from the roost and territory. Similarly, an injured jackdaw may be mobbed and then killed.

Nests are built by dropping sticks on a narrow crevice and building upon that. Chimneys are a favourite in the urban environment, and it has been the case that a nest has fallen down into a chimney, even with the birds still on it! Jackdaws have built nests in the lintels of Stonehenge, as reported by Gilbert White in *The Natural History of Selborne*, first published in 1789. The jackdaw can displace the tawny owl and the Cornish chough from their nests, but in turn, is ousted by larger members of the crow family, such as the magpie, rook or carrion crow.

Once the sticks are in place, the nest is made comfortable with wool, grass and hair. The female sits on the eggs until they hatch, in up to 18 days. Chicks take a further 30 to 35 days to fledge, being fed by the parents for an additional month. If food is in short supply, the last chick may be allowed to die. If the brood does not survive, another set of eggs is seldom produced.

The jackdaw feeds on small insects that are located above the ground, such as snails and spiders, cockchafers, weevil larvae, moths and butterflies. They also consume mice, voles, bats, bird eggs and chicks, and will feed on dead meat from the road. They enjoy grains from cereal crops, fruits such as elderberries, and seeds from common weeds. Vegetation makes up over 80% of their diet, apart from when feeding young, when insects form the majority. They will eat grit to aid digestion. Behaviour such as jumping, pecking, digging and probing the soil are common. They catch flying ants in mid-air and will swoop on cow pats to eat the insects. They do not tend to dig for earthworms from the soil but will wait until the field has been ploughed. They are known to sit on the back of sheep, eating ticks and collecting wool for their nest. The jackdaw's bill is less 'bent' than other members of the crow family, so it is able to use it to greater effect foraging on the ground. The bird shares its food, more so than for other species, including the chimpanzee. It is thought that the act of giving food, especially favourite food, reinforces the status of the individual within the community.

When milk was delivered to the doorstep, jackdaws would peck at the foil lid to gain access to the contents. In doing so, they contaminated the milk, which led to Campylobacter gastroenteritis in some parts of the UK. In Spain, people have died from stomach and intestinal problems, linked to infection by the jackdaw.

After several bad harvests, Henry VIII set up the Vermin Act of 1532, 'ordeyned to dystroye Choughes [jackdaws], Crowes and Rokes,' who were stealing his grain. Elizabeth I introduced the Preservation of Grayne Act in 1566, and jackdaws have been widely culled up until the middle of the twentieth century because of their grain-stealing behaviour. They have also been exterminated where gamebirds nest, as they take the eggs.

In the UK, the jackdaw is still considered a pest. It is legal to trap it in a cage, along with other members of the crow family, such as the jay, magpie or rook.

Juniper

Junipers are conifers belonging to the genus *Juniperus* in the family Cupressaceae. They have the greatest geographical distribution of all woody plants. The 52 to 67 species (depending on taxonomic perspective) are found throughout the world, from the Arctic to tropical Africa, as well as creating one of the highest tree lines on the planet, at an altitude of 4,900 metres in the Himalayas. Various species have evolved in response to different climatic conditions.

Juniperus communis, the type frequently found in the UK, is an evergreen tree or prostate shrub, growing up to 6 metres depending on the location. Leaves are spiny, whorling in clusters of three. They do not exhibit an 'adult' state, instead retaining their juvenile foliage. Plants are dioecious – showing both male and female cones, which are pollinated by the wind.

Junipers are gymnosperms, in that they have seeds unprotected by an ovary or fruit, similar to conifers, cycads, and ginkgo. These seeds, (commonly called 'berries') start life as green cones, which over an 18-month period become a blue waxy sphere. They are 4 to 12mm wide and are eaten and dispersed by birds in their droppings. The berries create a brown dye.

Oil made from juniper berry is rich in monoterpenes, such as myrcene, sabinene and limonene. The essential oil is utilised as a digestive aid, to help against respiratory infection, muscle ache and fatigue. Native Americans believed that juniper berries acted as a contraceptive for women. In Europe, juniper berries were historically used to fight the plague, soothe animal bites and cure poisoning. Ancient Egyptians used juniper oil, as well as other oils, to mummify and preserve the deceased.

Juniper wood is not large enough to use structurally; however, it finds a function in Scandinavia for containing dairy products e.g. cheese and butter, and is fashioned into the handles for butter knives and other eating utensils across the Continent. It has beautiful growth rings, and due to its slow growth, is strong and dense.

Juniper berries taste bitter when raw and are therefore commonly crushed and dried to add flavour to stuffing, meat and sauces. They tend to be used with game meats with a strong taste, such as venison, pheasant and rabbit.

The word 'gin' comes from an Old French word for 'juniper' and the berries have been used throughout Europe for centuries to flavour gin and other alcoholic drinks, such as the Finnish ale, Sahti; the Slovakian Borovička and the Dutch Jenever.

THE SECRET LIFE OF AN ARABLE FIELD

Kestrel

The common kestrel, *Falco tinnunculus*, is a member of the falcon family, and is found throughout Europe, Africa, Asia and occasionally eastern parts of North America. Falco comes from the Latin word, *falcis*, meaning sickle, referring to the bird's sharp claws. *Tinnunculus* comes from the Latin for shrill. The common name, kestrel, comes from the French 'crécerelle'.

Kestrels are small birds of prey, 33 to 39cm in length, with a wingspan of 65 to 80cm. Males are more compact than the females, weighing in the region of 155g, compared to 185g for the female. They have pale chestnut feathering, with dark spots above, and buff colouring with darker streaks below. The female shows greater streaking and black colouration than the male, the latter also having a greyish head and tail.

The kestrel likes open habitats in the lowlands, for example heaths, fields and scrub, as long as there are enough perching and nesting sites, and where plant life supports the required prey. Kestrels have been known to nest in central London.

The kestrel hovers around 10 to 20m in the air whilst hunting, using wind currents to soar. Their acute eyesight enables them to pick out prey from a great distance, and they dive towards it. Since they pick up ultraviolet light, they are able to perceive urine deposits and animals in their burrows. They can also hunt nearer the ground, watching from a post, whilst their prey scurries unknowingly by.

Prey includes small mammals, such as voles, mice and shrews, which account for 75% of the kestrel's diet. They will take fledgling birds in the summer, and more rarely bats and frogs. Earthworms, beetles and larger insects are also eaten. They have massive food requirements: depending on the time of year, they need around four to eight voles a day in order to stay healthy.

Breeding in the UK begins in April/May, with preferred nesting sites situated in cavities in trees, cliffs or buildings. Three to seven eggs are laid, buff coloured, with brown spots. The female will incubate them for around four weeks, with the male feeding her during this time. After the chicks are born, both parents provide food until they fledge four to five weeks later. These juveniles are able to reproduce the following year.

From this clutch, in the UK generally only two to three chicks will survive. Although records show that kestrels can live to 16 or even up to 24 years, 70% will not live to be a year old. Fluctuating prey populations, especially voles, have a hand in this.

The common kestrel is thought to share ancestors with the Australian kestrel, *F. cenchroides*, which probably diverged from *F. tinnunculus* about a million years ago. Kestrels seem to have evolved in the tropical forests of east Africa, 2.5 to 2 million years ago. Some of their prey species alive at the last Ice Age, such as the European pine vole, have accompanied them on this journey.

Historically, the kestrel was used as bait in Persia and Arabia to trap bigger birds of prey. Also, in Arabia greyhounds would be taught to hunt gazelles, by allowing them to chase jerboa-rats, whilst released kestrels would force the hounds to weave their way around the movements of the bird, thus replicating the zigzag tactics of the gazelle.

Kestrel numbers are down by 35% in the UK from the 1970s, due to changes in farming. There are thought to be 46,000 breeding pairs.

Ladybird

Gardeners love the seven-spot ladybird, *Coccinella septempunctata*, as it has such an appetite for aphids. Ladybirds are widespread throughout the UK, being found on grassland, heath and moorland, farmland, wetlands, woodland and in towns and gardens.

This much-loved beetle grows to 6 to 8mm in length and can be spotted between March and October. They overwinter as adults in cavities and spaces in plant stems, occasionally clustering. Every spring, large numbers of this insect will fly over to the UK from Europe.

The seven-spot ladybird is a familiar sight with its red wings, decorated by seven black spots, and a black and white body. These vivid colours serve as a warning signal to predators such as birds, spiders and larger beetles. Ladybirds also emit a foul-smelling liquid when handled.

Adults mate in May, with the female laying 40 eggs in small clusters on leaves between June and July. The ladybird goes through four life phases: the egg, larva, pupa and adult. Larvae are a browny-grey, with eight orange spots on their body. Throughout the latter three life phases, the majority of the ladybird's diet is aphids, with each bug consuming over 5,000 during the year that they are alive.

Lapwing

The northern lapwing, *Vanellus vanellus*, also known as the peewit or green plover, is found throughout Eurasia. They are seen in the UK all year round, leaving higher ground after breeding, and moving to lowland fields for the winter. Additionally, there are the birds from further north which migrate to the UK during the autumn. They migrate in large flocks from the northern most parts of their range, sometimes to as far afield as north Africa, Pakistan and India and China. After severe storms they can even be found in North America.

Lapwings in the UK prefer farmland. Cereal crops, root crops, pasture and fallow fields are their favoured habitats for breeding, especially in the north of England, the Borders and the east of Scotland. During the winter they flock to lowland arable and pasture land further south, and are especially numerous in the mud-flats of the Somerset Levels, the Wash and Morecambe Bay.

They are 28 to 31cm long, with a wingspan of 82 to 87cm, and weighing 140 to 320g. There are thought to be 140,000 breeding pairs in the UK, and an overwintering population of 650,000 birds. Males have a long, black, crest on their head, with a

black throat and white underbelly, and resplendent green tinted back. Females and juveniles have similar markings, with a shorter crest.

Nests are a simple scrape on slightly raised ground, lined in grass. Eggs are brown with black spots, which easily blend into the landscape.

The lapwing feeds on worms, insects, and pests such as leatherjackets and wireworms, making them popular amongst farmers. However, insecticides and farm machinery, which crushes nests, mean that these lapwings now usually breed on pastures and marshes.

The male's territorial flight is remarkable for its gradual rise, followed by a rapid, twisting dive, finishing in an upward twist. Their shrill call, 'pee-wit' lends itself to their common name. Their Latin name comes from the word *vannus*, meaning winnowing fan.

Numbers have declined by 58% in the UK from 1970 to 2007 due to habitat loss and intensive agriculture. Mammal predators have always been a threat. 'Plover's eggs' were once a luxury in Victorian Europe, although gathering these eggs is now forbidden. Over the last century, as a result of climate change, lapwings are laying their eggs earlier each year.

THE SECRET LIFE OF AN ARABLE FIELD

Linnet

The linnet, *Linaria cannabina*, belongs to the finch family. Flax seeds were once thought to be its favourite food, and its name comes from the word 'lin', which is the Old English term for flax. Linen is made from the flax plant. The bird also favours hemp seeds, and the species name, *cannabina*, is derived from the Latin word for hemp.

Seven recognised subspecies of linnet breed throughout Europe, north Africa and west Asia. They are predominantly resident, but in northerly and eastern regions of this range, birds will migrate. They are seen throughout the year in the UK, with the exception of the north of Scotland. Large groups of linnets flock in winter with other seed-eating birds on stubble fields, heathland and salt marshes. They favour the small to medium sized seed found in arable fields and in weeds such as knotgrass, dandelions, thistle, groundsel, as well as hawthorn and birch. They also eat a small number of invertebrates.

Predominantly due to agricultural intensification, herbicide use, scrub removal and hedge trimming, which all decrease their food supply, linnet numbers have dropped by 58% in the UK during the period 1970 to 2007. As a result, the linnet is protected by UK law, in the Wildlife and Countryside Act 1981. Across Europe, numbers have fallen by 62% between 1980 and 2009.

Measures to increase the linnet population include: overwintering stubble; allowing field margins and ditches to remain wild; planting seed-producing plants such as kale, mustard and oil-seed rape; and preserving hedgerows, especially those with thick cover.

The male has pink markings on his head and chest with a brown back and grey head. Females and juveniles do not have the pink colouring, being duller with increased streaks. Adults are 14cm long with a wingspan of 24cm. They weigh in the region of 19g and have a lifespan of 2 years.

The female builds a small, bowl-shaped nest in mid-April, in open land with thick hedgerows, often in gorse or brambles, a metre or so from the ground. She lays four to six blue/white eggs with purple specks, incubating them for 10 to 14 days. Once hatched, both parents feed the chicks with seeds and small insects. They fledge in a fortnight.

They have a beautiful song, particularly in the breeding season, and were once widely caged for this purpose.

THE SECRET LIFE OF AN ARABLE FIELD

Marbled White Butterfly

The marbled white butterfly, *Melangaria galathea*, is widespread throughout western and central Europe and into north Africa and western Asia, often found in colonies. In the UK it is limited to England and Wales, where it has seen a 30% increase since the 1970s.

It enjoys unimproved grassland, meadows, downland and roadside verges. The caterpillar feeds on grasses such as red fescue, sheep's fescue and Yorkshire fog. Purple flowers of wild marjoram, field scabious, thistles and knapweed are favourite foods for the adult. The butterfly tends to roost on the stems of long grass.

It is a medium size butterfly, with a wingspan of 50 to 60mm, and is a member of the Satyrinae, or satyr and brown family. The black and white pattern, shown by both males and females on the upperwings is very distinctive. Females are differentiated by their yellowish rear underwing.

Meadow Brown Butterfly

The meadow brown butterfly, *Maniola jurtina*, has a widespread distribution, covering all of Europe, parts of Asia (including the Himalayan foothills), North Africa and segments of the Arabian Peninsula, including Iran and Iraq. It thrives in areas south of 62°N. (Edinburgh is 55°N, whilst London is 51°N.)

The butterfly's range incorporates habitats such as forest edges, grassland, woodland and gardens. It is capable of living up to 2,000m above sea level. It is the most common butterfly in Britain, and unlike other butterflies, it will fly even on cold days in the drizzle. A number of subspecies have evolved due to its wide range of habitats.

Meadow brown butterflies exhibit distinct sexual dimorphism, with females appearing more noticeably orange on the forewings, whilst males are browner. This is unusual amongst butterflies as males are normally brighter. Carl Linnaeus, the Swedish naturalist, originally classified the two genders as different species when he was compiling his *Systema Naturae* in the seventeenth century. Their wingspan is roughly 50mm; females tend to be larger, exhibiting bigger false eyes on their forewings. These act to startle predators, giving the butterfly a chance to escape. The species has one generation, or complete cycle, a year, emerging throughout spring, summer and into autumn. They are able to do this as some larvae develop more quickly than others, giving a longer overall season. The adult life-span is around a month.

Meadow browns reproduce by depositing upright, ribbed eggs on a blade of grass. This egg starts life a white/green colour, deepening to brown/yellow. The emerging caterpillar will be a vivid green, with short white hairs and a darker stripe along its back. The caterpillar develops over six to nine months, eating a selection of different grasses, such as rough meadow grass, smooth meadow grass, *Festuca* species, *Agrostis* species, as well as false brome, downy oat grass and cock's foot. Adult butterflies enjoy the nectar from a wide variety of wildflowers, such as knapweed, dandelion, blackberries, groundsel, scabious, yarrow, thistle, heather, cow parsley, hogweed, oregano and privet.

Meadow Buttercup

The meadow buttercup, *Ranunculus acris*, is seen throughout temperate Eurasia. It is an herbaceous perennial, growing to 50 to 70mm high, with vivid yellow flowers that are 25mm wide. These flowers are made up of five petals, protected by five green sepals, which turn yellow with age. It has compound foliage, in three parts. Unlike the creeping buttercup, *Ranunculus repens*, its terminal leaflet is sessile i.e. attached directly to the base, without a stalk. The rare autumn buttercup, *Ranunculus aestivalis*, is very similar, but is only found in the US. The meadow buttercup holds a number of seeds in achenes, which are dispersed by wind, water, birds, rodents and other animals.

The plant is considered a weed outside its native range, particularly in New Zealand, where it can colonise a pasture, turning it into a sea of yellow. Animals avoid it, as the chemical protoanemonin in its sap is poisonous. So far, it has managed to resist herbicides. However, it is welcomed in wildflower meadows.

The Native Americans used to grind the plants to treat headaches or for use as a sedative, with some tribes using the roots to combat diarrhoea.

Meadow Sweet

Meadow sweet, *Filipendula ulmaria*, is a perennial herb in the Rosaceae family. It grows to a height of 1.25 metres, with strong, sweet smelling flowers that are held in cymes, on furrowed, reddish-purple stems. Pinnate leaves are dark green above, and downy white below. The flowers are creamy-white, small and plentiful, with 7 to 20 stamens encapsulated by five petals.

Also known as 'queen of the meadow', it grows in wet areas, such as ditches, damp meadows and riverbanks. Flowering from June to September, the plant is native to Europe and west Asia and has found its way to North America.

Historically, meadow sweet was used to flavour wine and beer, as well as vinegars and jam. Bronze Age remains from Carmarthenshire show meadow sweet in the stomachs of three cremated people. Chaucer (1340s to 1400) mentions the plant in *The Knight's Tale*, referring to it as mead wort, an ingredient of mead. Nicholas Culpepper, in 1652, wrote about the healing effects of the plant on the digestive system.

It was not until 1838 that salicylic acid was derived from the petals and buds. Salicin, procured from this, was used to make aspirin in 1897 by Felix Hoffmann. The plant was used traditionally for cancer, tumours and rheumatism, as well as respiratory infections and indigestion.

These aromatic flowers have been used in the past for weddings and garlands. Queen Elizabeth I favoured meadow sweet in the 1500s, to spread on the floor to hide smells and infections. If the flowers are crushed, they give off an antiseptic smell.

Medlar

The medlar tree, *Mespilus germanica*, is more often seen as a shrub, although it can grow to a tree of 8 metres in slightly acidic soil with mild winters and warm summers. The plant has a short lifespan of 30 to 50 years. The medlar fruit ripens in winter and has been cultivated for 3,000 years. It originated in Persia, in what we now know as Iran, as well as southwest Asia and southeast Europe, especially in Turkey and Bulgaria, where it favoured the coasts along the Black Sea.

Medlar has a deeply furrowed, grey-brown bark. Leaves are dark green and elliptic (oval shaped). These leaves are heavily haired and will flush red before dropping in autumn. Flowers are 6cm in diameter and white, with five oval petals. They blossom towards the end of spring and are hermaphroditic, containing both male and female sexual organs, pollinated by bees.

The brown-red fruit, 2 to 3cm wide, is a pome, in that it has a large, fleshy receptacle and a hard core which holds the seeds. Other examples of pomes include the pear, apple and quince. The fruit has sepals encircling the centre, making it look hollow. The fleshy fruit undergoes the process of bletting, which is the precursor for

ripening. Medlars can be eaten raw only after bletting, which is when the flesh colour changes from white to brown. Bletting can occur naturally with frost, or by storing the fruit for some time. The ripened fruit skin will wrinkle and darken in colour. It is very tasty with wine and cheese or added to yoghurt. It has a thickness and taste along the lines of apple sauce.

The medlar found its way to Greece in 700bc, and the Romans were enjoying it by 200bc. But its popularity was to wane in favour of other fruits, although its winter ripening still proves a popular trait today. Cultivars have been developed specifically for their fruit, such as Hollandia and Nottingham, the latter of which won the Royal Horticultural Society's Award of Garden Merit. Particularly large fruit can be found on the cultivars Royal, Large Russian and Dutch. Grafting the medlar on the rootstock of more adaptable plants, such as pear, hawthorn and quince will improve its performance in soils which it would not naturally take to.

Mistletoe

The European mistletoe, *Viscum album*, is native to Britain, large expanses of Europe, and western and southern Asia. It was originally placed by Carl Linnaeus in the mistletoe, or Viscaceae family. This family is currently taxonomically under debate and may be absorbed into the Santalaceae family. *Viscum album* has smooth-edged, evergreen leaves which grow in opposite pairs, up the woody stem, with white, milky berries that gather in groups of two to six. The European mistletoe was introduced to the US in 1900. Mistletoe is especially prevalent in tropical and subtropical regions; for example, there are 86 species native to Australia.

As a parasite species, mistletoe lives on a large number of different species of trees, resulting in damage to the host. It causes stunted growth and even death to the incumbent tree. Mistletoe gains most of its nutritional needs from the host plant. It is technically designated a hemiparasite – since they do photosynthesis themselves at some point during their life cycle. Mistletoe favours the tree-tops of broadleaved species, especially apple, poplar, hawthorn and lime.

Mistletoe has stems which are 30 to 100cm in length, with dichotomous branching, i.e. the terminal bud divides equally. Its leaves are arranged oppositely and have a thick texture. They are 2 to 8cm in length, less than 2.5cm wide and are yellow/green in colour. Mistletoe is dioecious, with male and female reproductive organs in separate individuals. The flowers are pollinated by insects and birds. These flowers are also yellow/green and tiny, at 2 to 3mm wide. The well-known white or yellow, waxy fruit is a berry, in which usually one seed is situated.

The mistle thrush and other birds enjoy the fruit of this plant. However, all parts of the plant are extremely toxic, and the berries have caused fatalities in humans. The problem is the viscumin that it contains: a protein that binds to certain sugars, causing some cells to stick together in a mass. This is a cytotoxic protein. Cytotoxic drugs are used to treat cancer, as they kill tumour cells by interfering with cell division. However, they disrupt normal cells as well, with serious side-effects.

Before Christianity arrived, mistletoe was regarded as symbolising the spiritual male essence, with attributes of love, potency and vigour. The Celts used it to cure lack of fertility in their livestock, and also to treat poisoning. The Roman philosopher, Pliny the Elder (23 to 79ad), tells of a druid clambering up an oak tree to cut some mistletoe with a golden scythe. Mistletoe rarely grows on oak, so it was a particularly

special occasion: part of a religious feast. The story was continued in the Asterix comic, *Asterix and the Golden Sickle*. The Romans considered mistletoe to bring peace and protection. It is not certain how the integration of mistletoe came into Christian symbolism, and it was not until the sixteenth century in England that kissing under the mistletoe was first documented. Using mistletoe as a Christmas decoration became widespread by the eighteenth century.

Croatian brandy is comprised of mistletoe ingredients. Herbalists use the leaves and young twigs to tend to circulatory and respiratory issues. Rudolf Steiner, the Austrian philosopher, was the first to recommend the plant in the cure of cancer, although its effectiveness is not proven. The waxy berries of mistletoe have been used as a sticking substance spread on to twigs to trap small animals or birds.

Mole

Moles are small mammals that live underground. In order to do so, they exhibit round bodies, with velvety fur that does not have a 'pile', tiny eyes and ears, diminished hind limbs and strong, robust forelimbs with large, shovel like paws evolved for moving earth. A male mole is called a boar, a female, a sow, and a collection of moles, a labour.

The term 'mole' refers not only to the 'true mole' members of the Talpidae family, found in Europe, North America and Asia, but also refers to insectivorous, digging animals, including shrew-moles and desmans, which are not true moles. Unrelated mammals, also referred to as moles, are found in Australia and southern regions of Africa, which have shown convergent evolution, i.e. independently, but with similar physical characteristics.

The term moldwarp has been in use since the Norman invasion of 1066, (when Middle English began to be spoken), until the late fifteenth century. By the Tudor period, from 1485 to 1603, Early Modern English had advanced this term, using connected German, Scandinavian and Icelandic words to give mouldywarp, mold meaning soil, and warp referring to the tossing of dirt. The expression, 'don't make a mountain out of a molehill' was first recorded in John Fox's, *The Book of Martyrs* in 1570.

Moles exhibit polydactyl front paws, meaning that they have a prepollex or additional thumb. This thumb is composed of a single bone, similar to that of a giant panda. The other digits are made up of multiple joints.

Moles consume large amounts of earthworms and small invertebrates. They also enjoy nuts. They are able to sense when a worm enters their tunnelling system and they can retrieve it very quickly. Moles act by paralysing their prey, using a toxin in their saliva. They store these invertebrates in underground larders, built especially for this use. Larders containing over a thousand invertebrates have been found. Before consumption, the mole will use their paws to compress the worm, pushing out the dirt and earth from its belly. Weasels and voles are known to use mole tunnels in order to eat plant roots, which the mole does not touch.

Moles are able to breathe underground as their blood contains a particular variety of haemoglobin that allows them to uptake oxygen from their exhaled air and thereby survive in oxygen starved conditions.

Moles are thought to be solitary mammals, only meeting to mate. However, territories can overlap and males are known to be extremely aggressive if they do meet.

152 THE SECRET LIFE OF AN ARABLE FIELD

Mole pelts are exceptionally velvety, a quality not seen in surface-dwelling mammals. They do not have a distinct pile, being so dense and short, all evolutionary characteristics to enable them to move around in small tunnels. Queen Alexandra, spouse to King Edward VII, created a trend when she ordered a mole coat, made up of hundreds of skins that had been cut into rectangles and sewn together. The colouration of a mole skin is taupe, coming from the French word 'taupe', meaning mole, although they can be dyed. The pelts for the Queen's coat originated in Scotland, where moles were a considerable pest, creating a profitable business, due to her status as a fashion icon.

Moles have a mixed reputation across the globe. Some countries think they are a serious pest, contaminating the quality of silage with soil, making it difficult for cattle to eat. Others complain about the yield reduction in a pasture, and broken farm machinery from uncovered stones. They are annoyed about the harm to plants, drainage systems and waterways. Germany, however, gives protected status to their moles, and they may only be destroyed with a permit.

Moles can be trapped with mole-catchers and smoke bombs. Poisons, e.g. calcium carbide, give off acetylene which the moles hate. Other gas controls include the use of aluminium phosphide, which fills the tunnel with phosphine gas. Nitrogen gas has begun to be used, as it does not harm the ecology.

The meat of a mole is vile, according to the Victorian, William Buckland, who claimed to have eaten his way through the animal kingdom: a process known as zoöphagy.

Mouse

The harvest mouse, *Micromys minutus*, is a small rodent indigenous to Europe and Asia. It inhabits fields where cereal crops such as wheat and oats are grown, also living in reed beds and in other areas where there is tall plant matter, such as long grass and hedgerows.

The harvest mouse has a reddish-brown coat, with a white underbelly and a long, prehensile tail, which is utilised for balancing when grasping and climbing plants. The tail is furless at the end. It possesses large feet, enabling it to climb, and its outer toe gives it the strength to grip stems, along with its tail, so that the front paws are available to obtain food. At 4g in weight it is the tiniest of European rodents. Its diet consists of seeds and insects, but it will also enjoy fruit and nectar. Its nest is a carefully constructed round ball of woven grass, raised above the ground and supported by stems.

The harvest mouse measures 5.5 to 7.5cm in length, with its tail making up a further 5 to 7.5cm. It can weigh from 4 to 11g, which is approximately half the mass of a house mouse (*Mus musculus*). Compared to the rest of its body it has quite substantial ears and eyes, with a small nose and whiskers. It will grow a thicker coat in winter to cope with the cold.

Harvest mice are preyed upon by cats, foxes, snakes and birds of prey and in some countries, by wild dogs and certain arthropods, such as spiders like the tarantula. However, the mouse is considered to be an extremely successful species, as it can adapt to almost any environment.

Gilbert White, the eighteenth century naturalist, described the harvest mouse at his home in Selborne, Hampshire: 'They never enter into houses; are carried into ricks and barns with the sheaves; abound in harvest; and build their nests amidst the straws of the corn above the ground, and sometimes in thistles. They breed as many as eight at a litter, in a little round nest composed of the blades of grass or wheat. One of these nests I procured this autumn, most artificially platted, and composed of the blades of wheat; perfectly round, and about the size of a cricket-ball. It was so compact and well-filled, that it would roll across the table without being discomposed, though it contained eight little mice that were naked and blind.'

Old tennis balls from Wimbledon have been used since 2001 to create artificial nests for harvest mice to help prevent predation of the species, which is becoming rarer in the UK.

THE SECRET LIFE OF AN ARABLE FIELD

Mice, generally, are still an important protein source in some parts of Africa. They have been consumed by early humans since before the first use of stone tools, about 2.6 million years ago. In Victorian times, fried mice were given to children to prevent bedwetting, and in the Second World War creamed mice were eaten as a result of food shortages. Mice are also kept as pets, and as food for snakes, lizards, birds of prey and frogs.

House mice are used as experimental animals in research labs as they exhibit a large degree of homology with humans. In other words, they have a similar gene structure. They are also inexpensive and easy to keep, breeding rapidly.

Muntjac

Muntjac deer are thought to have been around for 15 to 30 million years, with fossils from the Miocene period found in France, Germany and Poland. They are a small deer, the present day species native to Asia in countries such as Sri Lanka, India, Vietnam, Myanmar, Indonesia, Taiwan and the south of China. They also inhabit regions at the foot of the Himalayas in Nepal and Bhutan, as well as some parts of Japan. Their name comes from the Latin form of the Dutch word, 'muntjak', which in itself is taken from the deer's name in Sudan, which is 'mēncēk'. The German zoologist and geographer, Zimmerman, first described the deer as *Cervus muntjac* in 1780.

THE SECRET LIFE OF AN ARABLE FIELD

Muntjacs were not native to Britain. They were introduced to Woburn Park in Bedfordshire in 1838 by John Russell Reeves, and are hence named Reeves' Muntjac. Several deer escaped, with some being deliberately released, and they have bred rapidly, spreading throughout England and Wales. It is thought that they will soon become the most prevalent deer in England. Some were found in Northern Ireland in 2009 and the Republic of Ireland in 2010, probably through human intervention.

They are a small, stocky deer, standing 40–55cm at the shoulder, with a head and body length of 90 to 110cm. Their tail is approximately 15cm and they weigh 10 to 20kg. Males exhibit short antlers, which are able to regrow. They fight other males for territory using their 'tusks', or canine teeth that point downwards and can cause a great deal of harm. These 'tusks' are not present in indigenous British deer, although they are seen in a pronounced form in the water deer of China and Korea.

Muntjacs are crepuscular, most active in the early morning and at dusk. They commonly bark loudly and are known as the barking deer. They inhabit woodland and scrub. In the tropical regions where they come from, they have no seasonal breeding season. This characteristic is carried on in the UK, with mating taking place all year round, helped by their ability to conceive just days after giving birth. Numbers continue to grow, with the British Deer Society reporting in 2016 notable northerly gains in range since the last census in 2011. They are a conservation hazard in the UK as they damage the ground flora of the woodlands where they live.

Nettle

The stinging nettle, often known as the common nettle, *Urtica dioica*, has at least six subspecies, two of which are found in Europe. *U.dioca* subsp. *dioca* contains stinging hairs, and is found in Europe, Asia and parts of north Africa. This European stinging nettle has been introduced to North and South America as well as Australia. The other subspecies native to Europe is *U.dioica* subsp. *galeopsifolia*, which does not have stinging hairs. It is known as the 'fen' or 'stingless' nettle. Two different species of nettle, the dwarf nettle, *U.urens*, and the Roman nettle, *U.pilulifera*, are also found in the UK.

The European stinging nettle grows 1 to 2m in height during the summer months, receding to ground level in the winter. Roots are horizontal underground stems, known as rhizomes, which send out lateral shoots and adventitious roots. They also exhibit stolons or runners, which connect the different plants underground. Both roots and stolons are vivid yellow. The stem is green, with 3 to 15cm leaves arranged oppositely up its length. These are serrated and heart-shaped. Small, green/brown flowers grow at the base of the leaves, where they join the stem. The leaves and stem both exhibit stinging hairs, which pierce the skin, releasing several chemicals.

This sting inflames the skin, and is often named 'contact urticaria', although by definition, this can cover other skin conditions too. The sting releases histamines and

serotonin as well as other chemicals, which have a burning effect on the skin. Creams containing antihistamines or hydrocortisone can be used to combat this effect. There is a long-established custom of using dock leaves to soothe the skin, and conveniently, these tend to grow alongside nettles.

The nettle is used as an analogy on tackling difficulty by Aesop's phrase, 'Gently touch a nettle and it'll sting you for your pains. Grasp it as a lad of mettle and soft as silk remains.'

Butterflies love nettles. Larvae of the peacock butterfly, comma or *Polygonia c-album*, and tortoiseshell feed solely on this plant. The red admiral caterpillar also feeds primarily on the nettle. Moth larvae, such as the angle shades, buff ermine, dot moth, the gothic moth, grey chi, grey pug, lesser broad-bordered yellow underwing, mouse moth, setaceous Hebrew character and the small angle shades can all be found feeding on the nettle in the British Isles. The ghost moth larvae enjoys its roots. The nettle encourages many insects into a garden, although animals avoid eating the plant due to its stinging leaves.

Nettles can be boiled, which removes their sting, and then used in various culinary dishes, such as soup, omelettes, herbal tea, pesto and to preserve cheese, e.g. the Cornish Yarg. They are rich in vitamins A and C, as well as high in iron, calcium, manganese and potassium. Nettles contain a large amount of protein: up to 25% of dry weight. Sugar can be used to release the flavour of the nettle and then lemon juice added to create a cordial. Beer can also be fermented from the leaves.

Nettles have been recorded for their medicinal qualities since the tenth century, when the Anglo-Saxon *Nine Herbs Charm* was written. The nettle is used today internally to aid kidney, gastrointestinal or urinary disorders, skin and cardiovascular problems and rheumatism and gout.

The history of the nettle in clothing goes back to a sash, made from the plant, found at the Bronze Age burial chamber at Whitehouse Hill in Dartmoor, Devon dating 3,500 years ago. Similar finds have been discovered in Denmark, with nettle sail cloth, paper and fishnets. Nettle textiles are created in the same way as linen. The Germans faced a shortage of cotton in the First World War and soldiers' uniforms were made extensively with nettles. As nettles do not require pesticides to grow, businesses across Europe are beginning to favour their production instead of cotton. Nettles can also be used to dye clothes, either yellow, using the roots, or green/yellow from the leaves. Indeed, nettle can be fed to laying hens to intensify the colour of the yolk.

Stinging nettles grow best with high levels of phosphorus and nitrogen in the soil, doing especially well on damp, aeriated soil. Nettles can be used in compost due to their ample nitrogen compounds and can also be converted into a good liquid fertiliser, containing high levels of magnesium, sulphur and iron. Nettles flourish in chicken runs, where other plants cannot cope with the manure. If you want to get rid of nettles, it is not a good idea to mow them as it increases their bulk; instead regularly turn over the soil and remove the roots.

Oak Bush Cricket

The oak bush cricket, *Meconema thalassinum*, is a native, well disguised, tree-living insect, commonly found in hedgerows, woods, grassland, gardens and parks between June and November. They favour the mature tree canopies of England and Wales.

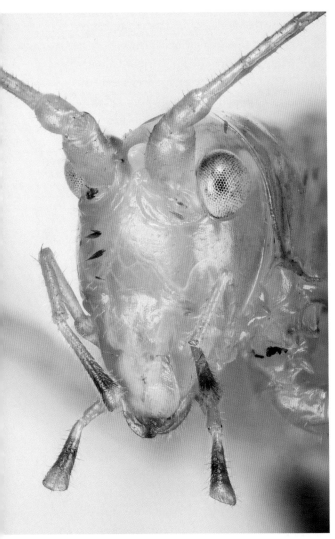

The crickets measure 14 to 17mm in length, with a slim, lime green body and a dark orange stripe located down their back. They do not have the black spotting of the speckled bush cricket. Males hit leaves with their back legs to make a sound that entices females, although this sound is rarely perceived by humans. The female deposits her eggs in tree bark in August. They hatch the following spring, and the insects go through five moulting stages before reaching the adult phase in early summer. Females can be differentiated from males as they have a lengthy ovipositor, (egg-laying tube), at their back end, whilst males have short, curved antenna-like organs.

Predators include birds, amphibians and reptiles. The oak bush cricket is a meat-eater, consuming small invertebrates like caterpillars. It is unusual for a cricket in that it does not rub its legs or wings in order to make the characteristic 'song'. The oak bush cricket can be spotted as they are attracted to lights at night.

THE SECRET LIFE OF AN ARABLE FIELD

Oak

The English Oak, *Quercus robur*, has held a special place in British hearts for centuries. This is not just because it can live for hundreds of years, and in maturity supports the greatest number of species than any other tree in the kingdom, but also because of its historic function in helping Britain rule the waves. The oak is indigenous to temperate and subtropical regions of Eurasia and has also been cultivated in North America and Australia.

It is a deciduous tree, growing up to 45m. The largest oak in the UK, in Newlands, Staffordshire, had a circumference of 13.5m before it fell. Nowadays, its crown has been taken by the 'Major Oak', deep in Sherwood Forest, which has a 10m girth, a weight of 23 tons and first started sprouting from an acorn 800 to 1,000 years ago. It is said to be the tree where Robin Hood gathered his men for meetings.

The oak's Latin name stems from *Quercus*, meaning 'oak', and *robur* denoting 'strength' in reference to its timber. Its wood is used extensively in construction and the making of furniture. So much so that Queen Elizabeth I made laws protecting the oak, to make sure supplies didn't run out. For centuries, up until the mid-1800s, oak was used to build the Navy, with particular emphasis on warships. There were eight battleships named HMS *Royal Oak*, and the Navy still quick marches to the song, *Heart of Oak*; indeed the Navy was referred to as 'The Wooden Walls of Old England'. The royal forests were extensively planted with oak saplings to provide for the Navy, with many of the trees still growing and enjoyed today.

Oak wood is used to manufacture casks for maturing wines and spirits, while the process of tanning leather utilises the bark.

Nearly 280 insect species make their home in the oak, making use of its thick and broken bark. This, in turn, supports a wide variety of bird life which feed on the insects. Almost 320 varieties of lichen have been found on the trees. Small mammals, such as dormice, make their nest in the tree, as well as bats, tawny owls and other birds.

Leaves fall in autumn, turning yellow, orange and brown before they do so. At the beginning of spring, moths deposit eggs which hatch just as the tree is coming into leaf again, providing a rich food source for the caterpillars. The oak will signal when enough is enough, by producing tannin in its leaves, which puts the caterpillar off its food. They then drop to the forest floor and begin pupating in the leaf litter, part of their natural life cycle. The oak exhibits lammas growth, in that it has a second flush

of leaf growth in August. Lammas Day, on August 1 is celebrated as the Celtic harvest festival.

Acorns will not develop on an oak until the tree is 25 to 40 years of age, and even then, it does not reach its productive maturity until 80 to 120 years. It will stop growing at the age of 250 to 350 years, with dieback in the branches and girth growth greatly reduced. An oak is thought to produce 10 million acorns in its lifespan.

These acorns are a vital link in the food chain for many wild creatures such as deer, badgers, squirrels, mice, pheasants, pigeons and jays. It is thanks to the jay that seeds are propagated so fully, as they hide them in the soil, away from the tree, and quite frequently forget where they have put them! The acorn will send out a large taproot and start to shoot in spring.

Acorns can be dangerous to cattle, sheep and horses because of the tannic and gallic acid they contain, which causes injury to the stomach, intestines and kidneys. Pigs used to be turned out in the autumn to eat the acorns, thereby protecting other livestock, in a practice called 'pannage' which is still in use by the 'commoners' of the New Forest today.

The oak has been the most populous tree in the UK for 5,000 years. It has been in Britain since the interglacial period 300,000 years ago. Famous oaks include the 'Royal Oak' at Boscobel House, in which the future Charles II took refuge to hide from the Roundheads in the English Civil War. This was after the Battle of Worcester in

1651 and Charles told Samuel Pepys several years later how he saw Cromwell's forces thrashing through the bushes below. When Charles regained his throne in 1660, he created a special Royal Oak Day on 29 May in thanks for his getaway. The Royal Oak is the third most popular pub name in the UK.

Another illustrious oak bearing a story is the now fallen Queen Elizabeth's Oak, which is thought to have begun life around 1100ad. It is steeped in legend: King Henry VIII and his second wife, Anne Boleyn, were said to have partied around it, and Queen Elizabeth I dined under it. The oaks in Bradgate Park, the childhood home of Lady Jane Grey, were said to be pollarded in 1554 as a mark of respect as she was beheaded in that year.

Other famous British oaks include Gog and Magog, over 2,000 years old, and located at the bottom of Glastonbury Tor in Somerset. They are believed to be the last remaining trees in an avenue of oaks which led up to the Tor itself.

Oats

The common oat, *Avena sativa*, is a cereal crop eaten both by humans and livestock. It is rich in nutrients that have been shown to lower cholesterol, although its avenin content can cause celiac disease in a small percentage of the population. It originated in the Fertile Crescent of the Middle East, from the wild oat, *A. sterilis*.

Oat crops have since spread across the globe, preferring a temperate climate, with cooler summers. They are able to tolerate more rainfall than cereals such as wheat and barley, and therefore are a popular crop in northwest Europe and are even grown in Iceland. The total world oat production in 2016 came to nearly 23 million tons, with the EU growing 8 million tons, with Russia and Canada following on, with 4.7 million tons and 3 million tons respectively. Oats can be planted in spring to harvest in early autumn, or in autumn for a late spring crop. The crop tolerates cold and frost but does not grow well in the heat of the summer.

Oats take up a large amount of nitrogen from the soil, and this needs to be replaced to ensure good height, quality and yield. The rampant growth of oats acts as a deterrent to most weeds; however tall, broadleaf weeds, such as wild mustard and goosegrass still persist. Oats are fairly disease resistant although they do suffer from leaf problems, for example leaf rust. Caterpillars, such as the setaceous Hebrew character moth, feed on the plant, but do not do much damage.

Harvesting occurs when the kernels contain 35% moisture, which is when they are beginning to turn cream. If the crop is left until it is completely ripe, there will be 10 to 15% losses as the grain falls to the floor during harvesting.

Oats are used to create oatmeal, or ground into flour to use in porridge, muesli, oatcakes and bread or as a thickener for soup. The first oat bread factory opened in the UK in 1899. China makes its staple food of noodles from the flour of *A. nuda*. Oats can also be used for brewing beer. In Latin America, a drink called 'avena' is created with oats and milk. Oliver Cromwell used to enjoy a hot oatmeal drink called a caudle, which was a blend of ale, oatmeal and spices.

Horses are widely fed oats to increase their energy, as are cattle, where the oats can be whole or ground into flour. Silage and hay are supplementary products made from immature oats, providing food for livestock. The crop can be used as a green fertilizer, by planting in winter and ploughing into the ground in spring. The stems of oat are used as straw for livestock bedding. It is valued as it is malleable, clean and absorptive.

Corn dollies are made from straw, and in the past straw was secured in a muslin bag to soften bath water. This quality still makes them popular in beauty products today. Medicinally, oats can help regulate menstruation and pains associated with it. They are also useful in treating urinary tract disorders and osteoporosis. The ability of oats to lower cholesterol, reducing the risk of heart disease, has made them a popular health food. They contain a wide range of nutrients and 100g of oats contain 20% or more of the recommended Daily Value of protein, many B vitamins, and minerals such as manganese. Rolled oats contain 67% carbohydrates, (of which 11% is dietary fibre and 4% is beta-glucans), fat makes up 7%, and protein 17%. It is the beta-glucans that are so good for cholesterol. In oat bran, levels of beta-glucans can rise up to 23%. Protein levels are the highest amongst all cereals, with a kernel of oat containing 12 to 15% protein, almost the same as soy protein and the same as meat, milk and egg protein.

However, 1% of the population of the developed world have a specific intolerance to some gluten proteins that contain prolamins. This causes celiac disease, the symptoms of which include abdominal pain and nausea, and which can lead to health complications, including cancers. The prolamins in oats are similar to the gliadins in wheat, the hordeins in barley and the secalins in rye. They are all glutens. The variety of oat is important when deciding on a gluten-free diet, with pure oats being made up of gluten of less than 20 parts per million. During production, including transport and storage, cross contamination of oats with other cereals is common.

Oil Seed Rape

Rape, *Brassica napus subsp. napus*, belongs to the mustard or cabbage family, Brassicaceae. It has vibrant yellow flowers and is farmed for its oil bearing seeds. Globally, this oil is the third biggest source of vegetable oil, after soybean and palm oil.

Rapeseed was one of the first plants to be widely cultivated by man, some 10,000 years ago. India saw its first crops 4,000 years ago, whilst China started growing rape 2,000 years ago. In Europe, (including the UK), and Asia, the plant is usually sown in autumn, since it needs the long, cold winter to start the germination process. It starts sprouting in spring, with seed pods maturing over a six to eight-week period until midsummer. A well-drained soil is favoured, with a pH of between 5.4 and 8.4.

The plant grows to 1m high, with flowers that are 18mm in diameter. These have four petals and sepals, with long, green seed pods that turn brown when ripe. The pods are made up of two separate sections, containing black seeds that harden when fully grown.

Rapeseed is used to make animal feed, vegetable oils and biodiesel fuel. It usually provides 42% oil, and the meal that remains is 43% unrefined protein. This protein rich by-product is fed to animals, particularly cattle, as well as pigs and poultry. The oil used to contain a 50% level of the unsaturated fatty acid, erucic acid, as well as a large proportion of the nutrient glucosinolates, which are found widely in the Brassicaceae family. Erucic acid can harm the heart muscles in animals, and with glucosinolates, were substantially reduced by breeding them out, allowing rape's utilisation for high protein animal feed from the 1980s onwards. Canola oil, which is trademarked in North America, contains less erucic acid, with levels of up to 5% regulated in the EU, and 2% in the US. Rapeseed oil on the market will contain these lower levels and is considered safe for infant and human consumption.

Rapeseed oil is expensive to manufacture into biodiesel. It is often combined with fossil-fuel diesel at levels of 2 to 20%. It is also implemented as a lubricant. In parts of Europe, it has superseded petrol for use as chainsaw oil. It also finds value in medicine, such as a moisturiser for artificial joints. The flowers of rape can cause hayfever and asthma.

Rape makes a useful cover crop, used widely in the US over the winter to halt soil erosion. Livestock can graze on most varieties after three months. Its biomass makes it applicable as a soil fertiliser, especially in China. Honeybees love the crop of rape. It produces a low fructose-to-glucose ratio in honey, which means it quickly turns into honeycomb. Beekeepers have about 24 hours to withdraw the honey once the

THE SECRET LIFE OF AN ARABLE FIELD

bees have covered it in their hives. Rape is predominantly wind-pollinated, but bee activity creates a large increase in yields. Birds, such as the linnet, sedge warbler and reed bunting eat the crop, as well as using it for nesting.

Rape suffers from various diseases, such as light leaf spot, which can split the stem, and canker, which causes a weakening of the stem over the winter. Pests, such as slugs and wood pigeons also feed on the plant, as well as insects such as the flea beetle, which ruins seedlings. The cabbage stem beetle eats the leaves, laying eggs in the stem, which their larvae then devour. The pollen beetle feeds on the flowers before they bud, and the cabbage seed weevil works its way into seed pods, depositing their eggs there. They do not cause a great deal of damage, but the holes that they make are utilised by the pod midge, which also lays eggs. Their maggots go on to eat the entire pod. However, on the whole, brassicas have very few specialised pests, due to their typical bitter taste. Glucosinolates break down to form mustard oil, which is toxic to insect life.

Both fungicides and insecticides are applied to the crop to protect it. Genetically modified rapeseed, tolerant to the herbicide glyphosate, was advanced in 1998, and has been widely taken up by Canada, which grew 90% of this variety by 2010.

Storing the seeds of rape requires some finesse. The tiny, round seeds make it dangerous to walk on stored seeds, and some people have been known to drown in them (although it is not as bad as linseed). They require shallow storage over the long-term as it is difficult to blow air into a great depth.

Around 70 million tons of rapeseed was produced globally in 2016, with the expectation that this will, with the development of biodiesel, increase further. Canada and China were the main producers, with yields of 18.5 and 15.4 million tons respectively. The UK produced 1.4 million tons in 2016.

Old Man's Beard

Old man's beard, or *Clematis vitalba*, belongs to the family Ranunculaceae. It is native to the UK and found throughout most of England and Wales, and up unto the highlands of Scotland. It favours damp conditions, an alkaline soil and higher summer temperatures, and it grows throughout the shrubberies and mountains of Europe.

It is a vigorous climber, which has caused significant problems in New Zealand, where it was introduced in the 1920s, and has subsequently been classified as an 'unwanted organism'. Its powerful growth suffocates native plants and the government is taking steps to eradicate it. With the absence of naturally occurring constraining species it has got out of hand. It climbs rapidly, bringing down tall trees and reducing forests to impenetrable low-growing infestations, which can be a particular problem in new plantations of trees.

C. vitabla has branched and grooved stems, which are noticeable by touch. Leaves are deciduous and the plant produces aromatic green/white flowers with feathery sepals. It is called by its common name as its fruits have elongated, soft projections,

which taken all together, resemble the fleecy appearance of an old man's beard. Seeds are pollinated by insects and spread by the wind. The plants are hermaphrodite, producing both male and female reproductive organs. They generate a small, dry, one-seeded fruit known as an achene.

The larvae of many moths feed on old man's beard, including the small emerald moth, the small waved umber moth and Haworth's pug moth, which all feed exclusively on the plant.

Remains have been found from the Stone Age in Switzerland, where old man's beard was used to make rope. Stems have been utilised across Europe in the past, for basket weaving and binding arable crops, being especially useful as mice do not nibble them.

Historically, old man's beard was used as a rootstock for ornamental clematis species, and reversions back to the rootstock have occurred. Seeds have also spread across continents by lorry, whose wheels pick up seeds from the road as they are driving. The plant has been introduced to North America and Australasia where it is a strong coloniser.

Orange Tip Butterfly

The orange tip butterfly, *Anthocharis cardamines*, is found across Europe, into Asia. In the UK it is widespread, with numbers increasing by 8% since the 1970s. It is found in light woodland, meadows and grassland, fenland, hedgerows and gardens.

The male stands out with his bright orange tipped forewings, which have brown borders and a single brown spot. The female lacks the orange colouration, instead being white with black wingtips. She has a larger central spot. Both genders have mottled, olive-green undersides, which help to conceal them whilst they are resting. The females bear a strong resemblance to female Bath white butterflies.

The orange tip is a medium sized butterfly, with a wingspan of 45 to 50mm. They belong to the Pieridae family; whites and sulphurs. They feed on vegetables in the Brassicaceae family, such as cuckoo flower and garlic mustard. Other brassicas, such as hedge mustard, winter cress, turnips, charlock, large bitter-cress and hairy rock-cress are also eaten. In the garden the female produces eggs from May to July on plants such as honesty and dame's-violet.

Ox-Eye Daisy

Ox-eye daisy, *Leucanthemum vulgare*, is a perennial herb of the family Anthemideae, found throughout Europe and temperate parts of Asia. It has been introduced to Australia, New Zealand and North America, where it has been cultivated horticulturally, only to escape from the garden. It enjoys growing in grasslands, roadsides, wastelands, under scrub and in open-canopy woodland, requiring an average rainfall of more than 750mm and heavy, damp soils. It thrives in disturbed ground, so much so that it is classified as an invasive species in over 40 nations.

The ox-eye daisy was first officially recorded by Jean-Baptiste Lamarck in 1778.

It is a tall plant, growing to 60cm, and spreads through its shallow, underground network of rhizomes. Near the ground, its stem will be hairy, but it lacks hairs further up. Leaves are larger at the base of the stem, up to 15cm long, reducing in size as you travel up the plant.

There are up to three flowers on each stem, which have a head of 3 to 5cm in diameter and 20 to 40 white petals, or ray florets. The central disc florets are vivid yellow, and the hairless green bracts holding the flower head are 7 to 10mm long. The ox-eye daisy flowers towards the end of spring to early summer.

A plant in full bloom can develop around 26,000 seeds and is one of the most productive pollen plants. These seeds find their way on and into animals, vehicles, crops and water, and are hard to eradicate as, for example, 40% are still viable having been ingested by cattle, 82% of buried seeds are viable for over 6 years, and 1% can still grow after 40 years. Cattle, however, do not like to consume the ox-eye daisy and

it spreads, reducing the surface area of their meadow. It out-competes indigenous plants, causing soil erosion and degradation of the organic matter in the soil. The plant can grow from even small fragments of its rhizomes.

Several crop diseases are hosted by the ox-eye daisy, such as the yellow dwarf virus in potato crops.

If you can't beat them, eat them! Flower buds can be marinated and eaten like capers. Maud Grieve, in her *Modern Herbal*, first published in 1931, explains that 'The taste of the dried herb is bitter and tingling, and the odour faintly resembles that of valerian.'

All daisies carry the risk of causing contact dermatitis.

THE SECRET LIFE OF AN ARABLE FIELD

Peacock Butterfly

The peacock butterfly, *Inachis io*, is found throughout Europe and in temperate regions of Asia. It favours grassy meadows, fields and open land, and is commonly seen on buddleia plants in the garden. Its larvae feed on the common nettle, as well as the dwarf nettle and hop. It has a widespread distribution, with a 15% rise in numbers in the last 50 years.

It is a large butterfly, with a wingspan of 60 to 70mm and is part of the *Nymphalid* family, or brushfoots.

The underside of this butterfly is mottled brown, which aided by the uneven edges to its wings, allows it to blend in to leaves when resting. The upperside of the wings is startling, with large eyespots. These alert the butterfly to danger, as birds are confused and try and jab at its wings, giving the butterfly time to escape, but quite often resulting in tattered wings.

Common Poppy

The common poppy, also known as the Flanders poppy, is a notorious annual herbaceous plant common in agricultural crops. It forms a natural seed bank within the soil, germinating as the earth is disturbed and flowers in the UK from May to October. Growing to a height of up to 70cm, there is a single bloom on each stem. These flowers can be 10cm in diameter, with four marginally overlapping petals, that are bright red, usually with black markings at their base. These flowers bloom only for a day, but each plant is capable of releasing 400 blooms each season in balmy weather. Rough hairs line the stem, at a 90° angle. The plant contains white latex, which is slightly poisonous to livestock.

It is found throughout the world, in Africa, temperate and tropical Asia, Europe and the Americas, blooming in fields, roadsides and grasslands. The plant has a long history, and no-one is quite certain where it originated from, but is thought to

Julia Johnson

have evolved with agriculture, being the most abundant crop weed. Simply put, its lifecycle works in unison with that of cereal crops, it is not affected to a large degree by pesticides, and it goes to seed before the harvest, establishing long-lived seed banks in the soil.

Poppies do not cause hay fever as they are not wind-pollinated. Their brightly coloured flowers attract insects instead.

Since the ground was so disturbed on the western front during the First World War, poppies grew in their thousands between the trench lines in no man's land. As a result, Poppy Day, or Remembrance Day, is held every year on 11 November to honour those who have fallen. Anzac Day in Australia and New Zealand on 25 April is also a time to commemorate their war dead with poppy wreaths.

The plant has been selectively bred to produce different colour flowers: for example, yellow, orange, white, pink and even black cultivars are on the market.

The black seeds are often used in bread but can be eaten on their own. Oil is also created from these seeds. The flowers produce a red dye, used in wines and medicines. The common poppy has been traditionally used as a mild sedative, as it holds the alkaloid, rhoeadine. It was used to treat gout and pain, as well as being formulated into syrup which helped children get to sleep.

Potatoes

The potato, which is the tuber of the plant *Solanum tuberosum*, is indigenous to the Americas and belongs to the family Solanaceae. Genetic testing shows that the potato was domesticated 6,000 to 9,000 years ago, in a region in south Peru and northwest Bolivia, even though it grew wild throughout the continent. Potatoes were the main food source for the Incas.

The Spanish brought the potato to Europe in the late sixteenth century, and it has become the fourth largest food crop in the world. Some 380 million tons of potatoes were grown globally in 2016, with China producing 99.2 million tons of that. Potatoes are credited with rapidly increasing the European population in the eighteenth century. Over 5,000 varieties now exist due to centuries of selective breeding, with 95% of these stemming from those found in the Chilean lowlands. The 250 wild species of potato are used in hybridisation to increase resistance to pests and disease. For example, *Solanum demissum*, found in Mexico, builds tolerance to the ruinous late blight disease.

The word 'potato' is a derivation of the Spanish, 'patata' which originally referenced the native Cuban word for sweet potato: 'batata', and the Quechua word for potato: 'papa'. In the sixteenth century, the herbalist, John Gerard, called them 'bastard potatoes' or 'Virginia potatoes', whilst the US call them 'Irish potatoes'. They are also commonly known as 'spuds', first documented in the 1840s in New Zealand. This name comes from the action of digging the ground to plant the potato, referencing a fifteenth century dagger, which is derived from the Spanish word for sword: 'espada'. The UK also borrowed this word to name their 'spade'.

The potato is an herbaceous perennial, growing to roughly 65cm, although there is a difference between varieties. Flowers are in a wide range of colours, with white flowers generally begetting a white tuber, whilst coloured flowers give a pink tuber. Self-fertilisation does occur, although pollinators are responsible for a lot of the work. Tubers are created as day length shortens. Fruits, formed after flowering, contain several hundred seeds. Potatoes like a cool, moist climate in which to grow. Unlike grain, they cannot be stored for long periods of time. They have a higher calorific count per hectare than grains or soybeans.

The UK farms about 80 varieties of potato. Russet potatoes have a brown skin, with red, white, gold and purple potatoes also available. Floury, or baking, potatoes contain slightly more starch (20 to 22%) compared to boiling potatoes (15 to 17%). Different colour skins give rise to varying levels of phytochemicals such as carotenoids, found in gold potatoes, and polyphenols, in red and blue. These chemicals are digested to give vitamin A, although anthocyanin, which colours red and blue potatoes and is also found in autumn leaves, does not appear to have any nutritional value. GM potatoes have been propagated, although they haven't caught on with consumers, and many food retailers refuse to use them.

The Great Irish Famine between 1845–9 also hit the Scottish Highlands. It was caused by a lack of genetic diversity in potato crops, making them susceptible to disease, in this case the airborne fungus *Phytophthora infestans*, or late blight.

Potatoes, when raw, consist of 79% water, 17% carbohydrates (of which 87% is starch), 2% protein and a minimal amount of fat. Good levels of vitamin B6 and vitamin C are also present, although cooking a potato will decrease these quantities as these vitamins are heat sensitive. These vitamins are also water-soluble, meaning that they may leach out when boiled. Potatoes have a high glycemic index (GI), which shows the relative rise in blood glucose two hours after eating. However, this is variable according to variety and cooking methods.

Glycoalkaloids are found in the green parts of the plant. These toxic substances which repel insect predators are also found in other poisonous plants, such as deadly nightshade and tobacco. The green parts of a potato, including green skins, hold a poisonous level of glycoalkaloids, which include solanine and chaconine. Cultivated varieties have bred this danger out, but poisoning cause headaches, diarrhoea, cramps and even death. Keeping potatoes in the fridge can prevent sunlight reacting with the chlorophyll, which gives the green colouring on the skin.

Seed potatoes, grown intentionally for propagation, should be able to resist disease. In the UK, a lot of seed potatoes are grown in Scotland, where winds from the west counteract aphid attack and the viruses associated with the crop. In the US, areas with cold winters and long, hot summers are selected.

Whilst growing, the potato will begin to sprout and send out roots. Leaves will develop, and stolons, or runners, form below the ground, growing into new tubers. The plant will send most of its energy to these developing tubers, allowing them to fill out. At this point it is vital that the plant remains pest and disease free. As the tubers reach maturity, the foliage dies back, having done its job, and the tuber's skin hardens, turning its sugars into starches.

Pests and diseases include the Colorado potato beetle, (now found across the US, Europe and parts of Asia), the potato tuber moth, aphids – such as the green peach aphid and potato aphid – as well as thrips and moths. The potato cyst nematode is a tiny worm that damages the tuber, and whose eggs can exist in the soil for several years. In the UK, the Soil Association has advised the application of a copper pesticide to curtail potato blight, even on organic farms.

A special tool called a 'grape' is used to harvest the crop, with three prongs and an elongated handle. Potatoes known as 'creamers' are harvested early, whilst they are still immature, due to their superb taste. Temperatures of 4°C, in a dark room, are required for long-term storage. Below this heat, the potato will start to convert its starch into sugars, which leads to a rise in acrylamide levels. This led to a global health concern in 2002, as this chemical is thought to be carcinogenic. Potatoes can be stored for nearly a year.

There are over 18.5 million hectares or 46 million acres of potato crops globally. However, yields can vary, with the developed world having access to more sophisticated pesticides and fertilisers, and with climate, seed quality and farm

management also affecting the crop. If developing countries raised their yields to the level enjoyed by the developed world, a further 400 million tons of the crop would be generated, more than the world's annual production.

Potatoes are eaten in many dishes such as fish and chips, roast dinners, shepherd's pie, bubble and squeak, bangers and mash etc., and other dishes found around the world. They can also be enjoyed in the manufacture of vodka and as livestock fodder. Potato starch finds many uses, as a soup thickener, in glue and for making paper. The US is looking at ways of using the polylactic acid in potatoes to make plastics. Starch products such as biodegradable packaging are being investigated. Potato skins are used to treat burns in India, with this quality being the subject of new scientific research.

Powdery Mildew

Powdery mildew is a fungus that forms on many different host plants. Belonging to the order Erysiphales, the most common is *Podosphaera xanthii*. Symptoms include white powdery markings on both leaf and stems, which go on to form spores. It usually grows in response to low humidity and average temperatures, severely damaging crop yields.

Powdery mildew needs a host in order to reproduce, both sexually and asexually. In asexual reproduction, spores are released which go on to cause further contamination. Each species requires different conditions to flourish. Wheat and barley pathogens tend to favour asexual means. Spores are passed on by woolly aphids, whose presence often indicates a later infection.

Powdery mildew is treated with regular application of fungicides, genetic means and cautious farming. In a home setting, milk can be diluted with water at a ratio of 1:10 and sprayed on the plant when it first shows signs of the disease. This is reportedly as effective as agricultural fungicides and is used to treat a range of plants such as pumpkins, roses and grapes. It is thought that the protein in milk oxidises in the sun to produce radicals which combat the fungus. Also in use, but not so efficient, are baking soda, vegetable and mineral oils, combined with water.

Potassium bicarbonate is used in organic farming, treating powdery mildew as well as apple scab.

Different powdery mildews affect different plants: for example, cereal crops are plagued by *Blumeria graminis*; legumes tend to be attacked by *Microsphaera diffusa*; onions fall prey to *Leveillula taurica*; whilst apples and pears suffer from *Podosphaera leucotricha*.

THE SECRET LIFE OF AN ARABLE FIELD

Primrose

The common primrose, *Primula vulgaris*, is a spring flowering perennial belonging to the family Primulaceae. It is found throughout western and southern Europe, the northwest of Africa and southwest Asia.

It takes its name from the Latin *primus*, meaning prime, denoting the fact that it is one of the first flowers to develop in spring. *Vulgaris* refers to the word common, indicating its extensive distribution.

The primrose grows 10 to 15cm tall with a ray-like arrangement of horizontally spreading leaves at the base of the low-growing plant. These leaves are evergreen, with flowers appearing from February to April.

It was Prime Minister Benjamin Disraeli's favourite plant, and the anniversary of his death, on April 19, is named Primrose Day in honour of him. The Conservative organisation, the Primrose League, formed in 1883, was named in his memory.

Primrose leaves are 5 to 25cm in length, measuring 2 to 6cm wide. They are deeply furrowed, with jagged crenate margins. These allow water to flow freely from the leaf in cases of extreme rainfall. A crenate leaf has one point to each vein tip, without any

points between the veins. The leaf slims towards the root of the plant where it joins a single stem which is burrowed deep in the leaf structure.

Flowers are 2 to 4cm wide, sprouting from thin stems and giving off a subtle aroma. They are usually yellow, occasionally white or pink. They are actinomorphic, in that they are radially symmetric, like other flowers such as the petunia, buttercup and wild rose.

Primroses produce a capsule, which opens to give small, black, sticky seeds. They are hermaphroditic, with each plant developing both male flowers, (thrum-eyed, with protruding stamens), and female flowers, (pin-eyed, with a distinctive style). Both male and female flowers are needed for fertilisation.

Primroses enjoy the nutrient and humus-rich, damp clay soils found in broadleaf woods and shaded hedgerows. They have suffered in the past from over-picking and are now protected under the Wildlife and Countryside Act of 1981, under section 13, part 1b, which states that it is illegal to intentionally uproot any wild plant.

Many insects visit the plant. Notable pollinators include, the *Bombylius* genus of flies and the *Meligethes* genus of beetles. The orders of Lepidoptera – butterflies and moths; Hymenoptera – sawflies; Coleoptera – beetles; and Diptera – true flies; as well as wasps, bees and ants, all play their part.

Ants spread the seeds, in a process known as myrmecochory, which is a mutualistic symbiotic relationship whereby the seeds have elaiosomes on their surface, rich in lipids and proteins. The ants convey the seeds to their nest and feed their young the elaiosome. They will then take the remaining seed to their waste site, which is highly fertile as it also contains deceased ants and detritus from their colony. The primrose seeds are able to put down their roots and increase their distribution.

The primrose has become a popular cottage garden plant, with cultivars developed in an extensive array of colours. The polyanthus is a hybrid between *Primula vulgaris x P. veris* (the cowslip). Primroses are propagated by seed or division.

The flowers and leaves of the primrose are eaten raw, although leaves can taste somewhat bitter. These leaves can be boiled into a soup with other plants or used for tea. Flowers can be made into wine.

Historically, the entire plant, including its roots, were used as a pain killer for muscle spasms, as a diuretic and for increasing the water content in mucus so that coughing could be more productive. It contains small quantities of saponins, (coming from the word *sapo* which means soap in Latin), which foam when shaken with water. These phytochemicals have a range of medicinal values, such as bringing down inflammation, strengthening the immune system and fighting bacteria. Their foaming ability also makes them useful in cosmetics, such as shampoos and soaps.

Rabbit

The European rabbit, *Oryctolagus cuniculus*, is not native to Britain. It was bought over by the Romans when they invaded in 43AD. Due to its reproductive rates it has spread rapidly throughout the land. Originally it came from southwest Europe in areas like Spain, France and Portugal, and parts of northwest Africa, for example Morocco and Algeria. It was hunted in its native range by predators such as the Iberian lynx and Spanish imperial eagle, but due to the rabbit's decline, these dependant species are suffering too. The European rabbit has been introduced to all continents with the exception of Antarctica.

There are no Celtic or Old English words for the rabbit, although the word 'coney' has been used since the thirteenth century to denote its pelt. The word 'warren' has roots in the Old English *wareine*, which itself has French roots. The rabbit used to be part of the *Lepus* genus, but was reassigned in 1874, due to several characteristics, such as dependant young, its skeletal configuration and burrowing nature. Molecular studies place the European rabbit as more closely aligned to the hispid hare and the riverine rabbit rather than the North American cottontails. Any resemblance with the latter is due to convergent evolution. The cottontail does not habitually construct their own burrows, and they have a different skull configuration. Fossils of the current European rabbit, dating back 500,000 years to the Middle Pleistocene period have been found. Six subspecies were recognised in 2005.

The rabbit is smaller than the brown hare, with no black tips to its ears. They measure up to 40cm in body length, with 8.5 to 10cm hind feet. Ears are in the region of 6.5 to 7.5cm long and they weigh 1.2 to 2kg. Their size will vary depending on food quality. For example, farmland rich in roots and clover will yield a bigger rabbit than those feeding purely on grass.

The rabbit's fur is grey-brown with a white or grey belly. Their characteristic tail with its white underside could act as a warning signal to other rabbits, showing when they flee from danger. They moult once a year in March, and their underfur will have regrown by autumn. Colour shade variations are common, with some black individuals seen.

The rabbit inhabits warrens, sharing with 2 to 10 others. They tend to stay very close to their burrow, only moving 25m away to feed and very occasionally 50m. If there is a strong food incentive, this may increase to 500m, but this is rare. As you can imagine, rabbits experiencing high predation will stay closer to their burrows.

They are very communal, with activity centred round the females in several burrow networks. Where the ground is easy to dig, social groups are looser. Both bucks and does show a hierarchal system, with bucks gaining power through their mating strength, and the dominant doe getting the best nesting chamber. She may have to fight other does for this. Death or severe injury is not uncommon. There is much at stake, as females lower in the pecking order have to make do with inferior breeding burrows, which often only have one entrance, making them very vulnerable to attack by fox or badger, especially as it will be away from the main warren. Reproductive burrows are a metre or so in length and are lined with grass, moss and the rabbit's own fur.

The dominant male will have several does, whilst subordinate rabbits of either sex will exhibit monogamy. Before mating, rabbits emit a smelly fluid through their chin glands with which they mark other rabbits and objects. Male rabbits, otherwise placid, can be extremely fierce towards each other during the prolonged mating season, which stretches from January to August. Each litter comprises three to seven kittens, but breeding is controlled in heavily dense populations by intrauterine resorption, where the embryos are reabsorbed into the womb.

Rabbits have a gestation period of 30 days, with does mating again as soon as they have given birth. Kittens are born with no hearing or sight and are practically hairless. They can see after 11 days, and it takes them 13 days to lift their ears. They venture out into the open after 18 days. Males are ready to reproduce at four months old, with females ready at three to five months.

Rabbits burrow on slopes to aid drainage. Openings to the warren will measure 10 to 15 cm in diameter and can easily be spotted, with the hole surrounded by excavated earth. Larger burrows may reach down several feet and are enlarged by successive generations. The work is done using the front feet, with earth being thrown backwards, with the hind feet kicking it further back. Usually, burrows are dug from outside in, but emergency exits may be produced when underground.

The rabbit is known to scream when in a state of high alarm. It grunts at fellow rabbits in happiness and growls when it feels threatened.

Rabbits are fond of green foods, especially grasses, in particular fescues. They enjoy crops such as winter wheat, but will limit their intake as they always have one eye out for a predator. Winter food favourites are tree bark, blackberries and acorns. They also nibble at root vegetables, such as parsnips and carrots. They can live for two to eight days without any food at all.

In their native range, rabbits face predation from a vast number of creatures, including foxes, wolves, lynxes, wolverines and dogs. Foxes and badgers are able to dig the kittens out, but a badger is too slow to chase an adult rabbit. Cats are also a threat. Scottish wildcats enjoy rabbits, which make up 90% of their diet. Ferrets, stoats and weasels are also out for the kill. This is all very stressful for the rabbit, and they have been known to die of fright, unwounded. The European polecat's feed is made up of 85% rabbit, and the mink is also known to benefit. Rats can prey on the kittens, attacking in groups from within the burrow. Birds of prey can kill rabbits, but it is only the bigger birds, such as the golden eagle and sea eagle, that are strong enough to pick them up in their talons. Smaller birds of prey, such as hawks and owls focus on the young.

The first documented account of rabbits as an invasive species came from the Balearic Islands, (now an archipelago of Spain), which had been invaded by the Romans in the first century BC. Records narrate huge crop damage, with falling trees and damaged houses as a result of the rabbits' burrowing. Emperor Augustus was called upon to help, and it is said that he sent ferrets.

Australia faced similar concerns after the introduction of the rabbit by estate owner Thomas Austin in Victoria in 1859. The country did not have enough natural predators and the rabbits swiftly bred, utilising the abundance of farmland and mild winters – which allowed it to breed all year, pushing out the native bilby. So much so, that between 1901 and 1907, a huge fence was built to stop their spread westward. However, this did not have the desired consequences, as the rabbit either jumped the fence or burrowed underneath. Matters were getting worse, so that in the 1950s the introduced virus *Myxomatosis cuniculi* curbed the spread of the rabbit population. It was not, however, effective in New Zealand, as the insects required to transmit the disease were absent. Rabbits in Australia today have achieved a certain level of immunity to myxomatosis and another fatal virus has been approved for use: rabbit hemorrhagic disease (RHD). This has already been used illegally in New Zealand.

The majority of domestic rabbits stem from the European rabbit, finding use either as a pet or as food. The Romans used to eat rabbit as a treat. Rabbits have been selectively bred since the Middle Ages to create both dwarf and giant breeds. There are 305 different breeds of domestic rabbit in over 70 countries in the world today. They have many purposes; for example, both Rex and Angora rabbits' fur is used to create a luxury yarn.

Two research centres conducted enquiries into wild rabbit behaviour in the 1960s. One of these was based in Pembrokeshire, where Ronald Lockley wrote, *The Private Life of a Rabbit*. This was widely used by Richard Adams in his creation of *Watership Down*. The other research centre was based in Australia, but since the widespread damage of myxomatosis little subsequent research has been carried out.

THE SECRET LIFE OF AN ARABLE FIELD

Ragwort

Ragwort, or *Jacobaea vulgaris*, belongs to the Asteraceae family, and is found throughout Eurasia, including India and Siberia. It has been introduced to the US, south America and north Africa. It has also been spread in Australia and New Zealand, where it is considered a noxious weed, with the law stating that farmers must remove it from their fields, often spraying it from helicopters. The plant favours waste lands, neglected pastures, railway embankments and roadsides.

Ragwort is toxic if eaten by cattle or horses, due to the presence of certain alkaloids. There can be a great deal of difference in alkaloid levels between plants, even those growing in close proximity. Animals tend to disregard ragwort due to its unpleasant taste. If a horse does consume ragwort in large enough quantities it will result in irreversible cirrhosis of the liver, with the horse showing symptoms such as low mood, yellow mucus membranes and lack of balance. It is thought that consumption of 4 to 8% of body weight will cause death in an animal. There is no known antidote to this poisoning, but it is essential to get the horse off the field. There are cases of a complete recovery. The toxins causing poisoning can also be found in animal feed, in the form of moulds. Ragwort leaves can contaminate hay, which will poison horses over several months.

The plant, ironically, is named after the patron saint of horses, St James, and it was once used as an equine medicine in small doses, said to cure a disease of the spinal cord and brain known as staggers. The Greeks and Romans created an aphrodisiac from the plant, called satyrion. The leaves and flowers can be used to make a green and yellow dye respectively. The Greeks also used the plant medicinally. Culpeper, in the seventeenth century, used the herb for the digestive system.

In the UK, the Weeds Act of 1959 named ragwort as an injurious weed, along with broad leaved dock, creeping thistle, curled dock and the spear thistle. This allowed the Secretary of State for Environment, Food and Rural Affairs to enforce by law, control of the spread of the weed on private land. Ragwort is the only toxic plant on this list, although, they are all damaging to agriculture. The Ragwort Control Act of 2003 placed further legislation on the control of ragwort.

Ragwort is biennial. However, if it is regularly grazed or mown, it may become perennial. Stems reach 0.3 to 2.0m with lobed leaves. These leaves emit a distasteful aroma, leading to its common names of stinking Willie and mare's fart. The name ragwort refers to the plant's ragged leaves. In Scotland, the plant is also called stinking Billy, not just from the odour of the leaves when bruised, but also referring to

William, the Duke of Cumberland, and his ruthless victory at the Battle of Culloden in 1746. Vivid yellow flowers are carried in closely-packed, flat-topped groups. They measure 1.5 to 2.5cm wide and contain both male and female parts, flowering for six months in the UK, from June to November.

Ragwort has been listed in the top 10 nectar producing plants in the Britain, and attracts a wide variety of flies, bees, butterflies and moths. It can develop thousands of flowers over the course of the summer and early autumn, each plant producing over 100,000 seeds annually. These seeds are spread by wind, water, animals and farm implements but they tend not to travel far, hence the high density of ragwort plants in any given area.

The black and yellow cinnabar moth caterpillar ingests the toxic alkaloids, and in doing so, becomes unpleasant in taste to predators, as is the black and red adult moth when it emerges, giving off its warning colours to signify this. This moth has been introduced as a useful ragwort control in the US and New Zealand, where farmers can easily identify them from their vibrant colours. The tansy ragwort flea beetle was introduced to the US in 1969 to control ragwort. A similar beetle, *Longitarsus ganglbaueri*, was also used, but as it feeds on other plants as well, it was not considered viable.

In the UK, over 77 insects use the plant for shelter and/or food. Of these, 30 feed solely on ragwort, with the plant being a very important source for another 22 species. English Nature identifies a further 117 species that use ragwort as they move between feeding or breeding sites, or groups of populations. At least 10 insects that feed exclusively on ragwort are listed as threatened or very rare, such as the picture winged fly, scarce clouded knot horn moth and Sussex emerald moth. The cinnabar moth, although widespread, is reported as rapidly declining in the UK. Ragwort is an important species in maintaining diversity in insect life and plays a valuable part in the eco-system, as long as it grows in the right place.

Red Campion

The red campion, *Silene dioica*, grows in the hedgerows, woodland, verges and grassland of Europe. This species is an ancient woodland indicator. It is seen in the UK from May to September, blooming once the bluebells have retreated. It is a biennial or perennial plant, growing up to a metre high, dying back in autumn. It is also commonly known as adder's flower, Robin Hood, or cuckoo flower.

Each flower is 18 to 25mm wide, with five deeply notched petals, fusing at the base. Plants are either male or female; the female producing fruit from July onwards. These fruit contain thousands of seeds. Flowers are unscented, but flies such as *Rhingia campestris* are very attracted to them, as are butterflies and bumblebees, for example the large white butterfly, which drinks the nectar. The hairy leaves, which grow in opposite pairs, provide food for a number of moth species.

Traditionally, compressed seeds were applied to snakebites.

Red Fox

The red fox, *Vulpes Vulpes*, can be found widely in the northern hemisphere, with a range of 70 million km², from Europe to North Africa, North America, and into most of Asia. It can be found in the UK in hedgerows, meadows, woodlands and even the garden shed. It does not occur in Greenland, Iceland, the Arctic Islands and northern Siberia. The red fox has been introduced to Australia, where it is regarded as invasive, endangering native species. In New Zealand it has been classified as a 'prohibited new organism' from 1996, under the Hazardous Substances and New Organisms Act.

There are at least 45 recognised subspecies which vary in size, with the more northern ones being the largest. The species is very family orientated, with young staying with their parents to assist in new litters. Food wise, rodents, such as voles and mice are the primary source of nourishment, although foxes supplement their diet by feeding on reptiles, rabbits, hares, game and songbirds and occasionally young deer and lambs. They also enjoy vegetation, for example grasses and tubers, and fruit, such as blackberries, apples and acorns. They hunt at dawn and dusk, alone, unless there are plentiful resources available. In the UK, golden eagles prey on foxes, and their kits are taken by badgers. In some European and North American regions, adult foxes will be killed by wolves, bears and coyotes.

The vixen is the female fox, and young are known as kits. The red fox goes back 1.8 to 3.4 million years ago, with fossil remains found from this period in Hungary. It is thought that ancient humans ate the meat and used the pelt of the fox. Foxes can travel great distances, some up to 200 miles a year. When running, they reach speeds of up to 30mph, and trot at 4 to 8mph. They can jump over 2m high and are capable swimmers. Vixens possess at least four teats, but usually more. There is a lot of geographical variation in size. The biggest fox documented in the UK was a 17.4kg male, measuring 1.4m in length, found in Aberdeenshire in 2012.

Foxes in the winter possess a long, silky and very dense fur. They get a summer coat, excluding the thermal windows of the head and lower legs, which is short and thick all year round. The tip of the tail is white, and there is often the pattern of a black cross present on their backs. When the vixen is caring for her kits, the fur on her abdomen becomes brick red.

Foxes have binocular vision, which means they see in three dimensions, being particularly acute to movement. Their hearing is also exceptional, allowing them

THE SECRET LIFE OF AN ARABLE FIELD

to determine the precise motion of bird flight at 0.5km, and pick up the sounds of squeaking mice at 100 metres. Foxes rely on their vision and hearing more than their sense of smell, locating their prey with sound, and then leaping forwards up to 5 metres to capture their target. They will fight to protect their bounty, even against more dominant animals. Foxes are capable of mass killings, such as with poultry and caged game birds.

Red foxes can either move about or settle in one area. They use urine to mark their territory, with twelve different methods of spraying. In family groups, there can be up to eight subordinate foxes, mainly juveniles, who help take care in raising the young, guarding them, playing and cleaning them and assisting in feeding. There is one litter of kits each year, in spring. The vixens' ovaries double in size in December, at which point the male is also ready to mate. Pairs copulate over the course of several days, leading to a gestation period of 50 to 58 days. If a subordinate vixen has a litter, they will be killed by other foxes in the group.

Usually four to six kits are born, more in an area of high mortality. The vixen stays with them for two to three weeks, while being fed by other foxes. They are blind and deaf, with no teeth, and require her presence to thermo-regulate. Starting off with blue eyes, these turn amber after a month, at which point kits will also be accepting solid food. They still take milk for a further few weeks, reaching adult size in six to seven months. Female kits are able to reproduce the following year. They can live to 15 years in captivity, but in the wild, usually no more than five years.

After breeding, foxes head out to their preferred habitat of open ground with dense vegetation, returning to their lair in bad weather. These tunnels, dug into a hill, or within tree roots, tend to be 6m in length, 2m below ground and with an entrance at 45°. Several side tunnels fan out in larger lairs. They occasionally share burrows with badgers but are not as clean as them; the foxes' burrow is often littered with carcasses.

Foxes communicate with body language and vocalisations which span five octaves. Twelve different sounds have been recorded for the adults, whilst kits make eight different noises.

Red foxes in Europe are rabies vectors, which mean they carry rabies without showing any of the symptoms. In London, foxes typically suffer from arthritis of the spine. They do not seem to have a problem with fleas, but mange is a cause for concern, originating from mites, leading to extensive hair and weight loss. Death follows, but not for several months.

Fox hunting has been recorded since 400BC. By the thirteenth century, King Edward I kept a pack of hounds and employed a fox huntsman, following the foxes above ground rather than sending terriers into their burrows. The Civil War in England, (1642 to 1651), saw a fall in deer numbers, resulting in fox hunting becoming very fashionable, so much so, that territories were drawn up, and the first club, the Charlton Hunt Club, near Goodwood, was formed in 1737.

UK foxes were exported to Maryland and Virginia in the 1730s for hunting by the affluent tobacco farmers. The red fox provided more sport than the native grey fox in the US, as it led the hunt on more of a chase, covering 30 miles in a day, whilst the grey fox would stay closer to home, perhaps covering five to six miles. The UK is reported to have killed nearly 25,000 foxes in 2000 before the Hunting Act was passed. Nowadays, it is thought that 100,000 foxes meet their death on the roads each year in the UK. The worldwide trade in red fox fur stood at 1.5 million pelts in 1985–6.

There are thought to be 15,000 foxes living in London. They grow bigger than rural foxes, as there is more food available, and fewer predators. The highest concentration of urban foxes is found in Bournemouth, with 23 foxes per square kilometer, compared to 18 in London and 16 in Bristol. They are instrumental in keeping down the rat and mice populations in the city.

THE SECRET LIFE OF AN ARABLE FIELD

Reed Bunting

The common reed bunting, *Emberiza schoeniclus*, breeds throughout Europe and most of temperate Asia. In the colder regions of this range, birds migrate south during the winter, although resident populations remain in milder areas. The UK has 200,000 resident breeding pairs, with migrants arriving in October. They are found across the UK, and as their name suggests, they inhabit reedbeds, as well as enjoying open farmland, forestry plantations and downland scrub.

The bird is 13 to 15cm long, with a small bill, designed to eat seeds. The male's head and throat are black, with a white band across the neck and white underbelly. His back plumage is streaked with brown. The female is less striking, with a brown streaked underbelly and head.

They build their nest in a bush, tussock or reeds, producing four to seven brown/olive eggs. Chicks hatch within two weeks and are dependent on both parents for a further fortnight. There are two to three broods each year. The birds eat insects when they are young, growing up to consume a more seed-based diet.

The common reed bunting in the UK has decreased by 27% from 1970 to 2007.

Ringlet Butterfly

The ringlet butterfly, *Aphantopus hyperantus*, has seen a massive surge in numbers since the 1970s, with UK populations increasing by nearly 65%. They are found across Europe and into Asia, enjoying woodland glades, hedgerows, roadside verges and open grassland, favouring areas with a little shade.

The ringlet is a typical member of the Satyridae family, composed of satyrs and browns. It is small butterfly, with a wingspan of 40 to 50mm, dark brown in colour, with a distinctive band of eyespots. These are especially visible on the paler underside of the wing. The spots are black, circled by yellow with a white accent. The number and distribution of these spots vary, and are thought to confound predators of the exact location of the ringlet's body. It can easily be mistaken for male meadow brown butterfly, which has similar markings.

Caterpillars munch on cock's foot, false broom, tufted hair-grass, common couch, meadow grasses and other coarse grasses. The butterfly will feed on nectar from the flowers of bramble and wild privet. They are known to fly in overcast conditions when other butterflies would not.

Rook

The rook, *Corvus frugilegus*, belongs to the crow family, and is found throughout Eurasia from Siberia to Scandinavia and the UK. Rooks are known for their sociable nature, forming rookeries, or communities of nests, high up in the trees. These nests are formed from a cup of sticks, strengthened by soil and lined with roots, moss, leaves, straw and wool. At Hatton Castle, Aberdeen, more than 6,000 nests have been counted in a single rookery.

Collective terms for rooks include a 'building', 'clamour', 'parliament' or a 'storytelling'. Its Latin name comes from the words, 'raven' and 'fruit-gathering', whereas its common name is related to its jarring call. Rooks are resident in the UK, meaning that they do not migrate; however, in the most severe northerly regions of Europe with a latitude of greater than 60°N, they will travel south over winter.

Their strong bills are perfectly adapted for probing soil-dwelling invertebrates on farmland and fields, whilst also eating cereal crops and plants. They dislike forests, swamps and moorland, and prefer the lowlands, usually occupying areas of 150m above sea level. They tend to settle near small populations of humans, requiring tall trees to nest. The scarecrow was one device historically used by farmers to drive them away, but these birds are intelligent and can problem solve.

Of the 60% plant matter that is eaten, most of it is cereals, potatoes, roots, acorns, berries and seeds. The remaining 40% is made up of earthworms, small birds and mammals, slugs and snails, insects and carrion. In urban environments, food from rubbish bins will be consumed after dark.

The bird is about 45cm long. Its black feathers glimmer blue/purple in the sunlight. Feet and legs are also black, but their beak is slightly grey and they have dark brown eyes. White, hairless skin is seen at the base of the bill and in front of the eye, which aids differentiation from other members of the crow family. Juveniles will lose feathering in these areas at about six months.

Their flight is straight with few wingbeats and not much gliding, although when socialising at the rookery the birds will glide and circle more. Flying as a group, they perform some wonderful acrobatic and parallel movements.

The nest is made by the female, with the male bringing the materials. He can break off small branches from trees, but often thieves from other nests to provide the twigs and lining. Mating couples stay together for life, within their flock. Jackdaws quite often join them when they get together at dusk to roost communally.

Before mating, a male rook will attract the attention of his female, by bowing to her and dropping his wings, whilst displaying his tail. She will lower her body in response and also erect her tail. They will then mate, which draws the attention of other males, who ambush the couple, trying to mate with the female. She hastily exits to a nearby branch. A mated couple will often fondle each other's beaks throughout the year.

There are usually three to five eggs in a clutch, sometimes up to seven, and in the UK, these are laid in March/April. The eggs are green/blue with heavy brown markings. The mother sits on them for 16 to 18 days, whilst her partner feeds her. Ten days after hatching, she will also start foraging. Chicks take 33 days to fledge, although both parents will still provide food for them. There is just one clutch of eggs per year.

Captive studies have shown that rooks can rival, if not outcompete, chimpanzees in intelligence and problem solving tests, although in the wild they do not exhibit tool use.

In 1424, James I of Scotland was angered by the damage the birds were doing to his crops, and ordered the eradication of all rooks. In 1532, Henry VIII acted in a similar fashion, bringing about the Vermin Act to 'dystroye Choughes, Crowes and Rokes'. In 1566, Elizabeth I established the Act for the Preservation of Grayne, which saw vast quantities of these birds destroyed. The practice of employing young children 'with hooting and crackers, and rattles of metal, and, finally throwing of stones, to scare them away,' was noted by the ornithologist Francis Willughby in 1678. What they did not realise was that the rooks, in eating the insect pests, were actually doing some good. However, the birds were more appreciated in the superlative rook and rabbit pie, but care had to be taken to get a young bird, as an older one was unpalatable.

Due to their widespread distribution, rooks are not considered endangered. Indeed, there has been a 41% increase in their population in the UK from 1970 to 2007.

Rowan

Rowan, also known as mountain ash, belongs to the genus *Sorbus*, in the rose family, Rosaceae. This genus enjoys cool temperate environments in the northern hemisphere, showing wide diversity, particularly in the mountainous regions of China and the Himalayas. Rowan's Latin name is *Sorbus aucuparia*, stemming from the words 'avis' meaning bird and 'capere' denoting catching, and explaining the use of its fruit for catching birds for the cooking pot. Its common name is derived from the fact that it grows higher up the mountain than other native trees, often seeding through bird's droppings. It shows a considerable degree of hardiness, growing as far north as Vardø, 70° North in arctic Norway. The tree has also been introduced successfully to North America.

Rowan is a small deciduous tree, growing to 10 to 20m, with some only making a shrub. They bear a similarity to the ash trees in the *Fraxinus* genus of the *Oleaceae* family, with incredibly similar leaf structure. However, the rowan has alternate leaves, where the leaves are single at each node and borne along the stem alternatively in an ascending sprial. The ash has opposite leaves, where the plants are paired at a node and borne opposite each other. Although there are similarities, the rowan should not be mistaken for *Fraxinus ornus*, which is a true ash, also known as 'mountain ash'.

Flowers are creamy white, and about 5 to 10mm in diameter, showing five petals. The fruit is smaller and a bright red pome, i.e. it has a fleshy receptacle with a hard centre which holds the seeds, like an apple or pear. Birds love this fruit, and waxwings and thrushes are eager visitors to the rowan. Bird-catchers once used the fruit as bait to trap redwings, thrushes and fieldfares. Butterfly and moth larvae also enjoy feeding on the fruit of a rowan, and the flowers are a source of pollen and nectar for insects.

Fruit of *Sorbus aucuparia* is used to make a jelly that is delicious with game. The bitter taste of the raw fruit can be remedied by either picking them after a frost, or by storing them in the freezer. Jams and preserves can also be cooked up with it. Rich in vitamin C, it was once made into a drink to prevent scurvy. It can be used as a coffee substitute, to flavour liqueurs and to make wine. Austrians create rowan schnapps and the Welsh rowan wine goes by the name *Diodgriafel*.

It does however contain both sorbic and parasorbic acid, the latter at levels of 0.4 to 0.7%. Parasorbic acid is responsible for indigestion, which can cause kidney damage. However, its toxicity can be abated by cooking the fruit, from whence it turns into the safe sorbic acid. Sorbic acid is widely used as a food preservative, credited with

making the global food chain feasible. It inhibits the growth of mould in foods and is also used in animal feeds, pharmaceutical drugs and cosmetics.

The rowan has strong, flexible, yellow-grey wood and in the past was utilised widely, making tool handles. It was frequently used instead of yew in the creation of longbows.

Until the Norman invasion in 1066, Old English was spoken, and the tree was named 'cwic-beám', translating to the present day as quickbeam. This was preceded by the earlier Scandinavian language, Norse, where the tree was named, 'runa', which translates as charm.

The tree has long been associated with witchcraft, lending protection against evil. An especially powerful rowan is said to be those which have grown in the boughs or holes of an oak or maple. These trees are known as an epiphyte to the larger tree, and termed a 'flying rowan'. A rowan was frequently planted outside houses and in graveyards to repel witches, and a May Day tradition was to hang a rowan sprig over doors and to decorate wells in order to banish evil.

The rowan tree's role in symbolism lends a hand to weather forecasting. Newfoundland residents claimed the rowan 'will not bear a heavy load of fruit and a heavy load of snow in the same year'. Other countries, such as Finland, believed that if there were plenty of flowers on the rowan, the rye crop would be huge.

Skylark

The Eurasian skylark, *Alauda arvensis*, has seen a 51% decline in numbers in the UK between the years 1970 to 2007. The birds belong to the Alaudidae family and are found throughout Europe and Asia on farmland and heath, grassland and commons, as well as mountainous regions in the north of Africa. Skylarks were introduced to Australia and New Zealand in the 1860s where they have thrived in cooler areas. Populations taken to the Hawaiian Islands in 1865 saw some success, whilst initiations on Vancouver Island, Canada have declined due to habitat destruction.

Skylarks in the UK do not migrate. However, further east, the birds will fly south in the winter to keep warm. A mass of skylarks is collectively known as an 'exaltation'. The species is easily recognised by the distinctive song of the male, hovering at 50 to 100m above the ground. The bird warbles for several minutes as it circles and swoops in the sky. During the mating season the male can sing for over 20 minutes. Both genders are brown, with a creamy body and darker streaks on the back. They measure around 18cm from head to tail, with a small crest on their heads.

Nests are created in hollows on open ground, at some distance from trees and undergrowth. The female lays three to five eggs, which are green/grey with olive/brown spots, taking 11 days to hatch. Both parents feed the emerging chicks with insects for 10 days. These chicks rootle around in the undergrowth for a further 10 days, from whence they can begin to fly. They are obviously very vulnerable to predation during this time. Skylarks produce a number of broods each year.

There are thought to be 11 subspecies of the Eurasian skylark throughout its range. The specific name, *arvensis*, translates from Latin to: 'of the field'. The skylark feeds whilst walking over the ground, eating insects, seeds and the new growth on plants. Skylarks are able to eat the grain in the husk, unlike a finch.

Farmers are now being asked to cater for the skylarks whilst sowing their fields. The RSPB has found that if the seed machine is stopped for five metre stretches when sowing, the skylark population increases, even if this creates only two skylark plots per hectare. New initiatives are being taken up by the UK government to create biodiversity in farmland. The RSPB maintain that the loss in numbers is only partly due to pesticides. Cereal crops are now being sown in the autumn, rather than the spring, which has a huge impact as it creates too dense an area for the bird to feed and nest in March or early April. The ideal vegetation height is between 25 and 50cm, The stubble that remains is described as a 'giant bird table'.

The verb, 'lark', was first used by sailors, to describe fooling around.

THE SECRET LIFE OF AN ARABLE FIELD

Sloe

The sloe, or blackthorn is a member of the Rosaceae, or rose family. It goes by the Latin name *Prunus spinosa* and is found throughout Europe, west Asia, north Africa as well as regions in New Zealand, Tasmania and eastern North America.

It can grow to a tree of 5 metres, but is also found as a shrub, being popular for hedging in cattle grazing areas, due to its sharp spur shoots. Blackthorn has a very dark bark and dense spiny branching. Leaves are oval, and flowers, when they appear in spring, are creamy white. The plant is hermaphroditic, containing both male and female sex characteristics, requiring insects for pollination. Sloes, the fruit of blackthorn, are technically drupes, in that they contain a stone. The quality of the sloes depends on the weather conditions during the previous spring and summer. They need water and warmth but if it is too wet the sloes do not develop, whereas if it is too dry, they will be small.

The usual time to pick sloes is during October or November in the UK, after the first frosts, at a time when they have naturally started to fall to the ground. The sloes

should squash between the fingers. The fruit will be quite astringent if eaten before the frosts. The liqueur, sloe gin, is a popular drink, made from immersing the berries in gin and sugar. Vodka can also be used. If the fruit is picked earlier, it is placed in the freezer to mimic the frosting period. This leads to the skin splitting so it is not necessary to individually prick all the berries.

The word 'sloe' has roots in Old English 'slāh', linked to the Old High German 'slēha' or 'slēwa' as well as many other cognations from other European countries. Across the Continent, sloes are utilised to make various liqueurs. Spain creates a drink known as pacharán. Italy creates bargnolino. France makes a wine, by infusing the initial shoots of spring with sugar. Indeed, wine, brewed with sloe berries, is a favourite across Europe. Chutney, jam and fruit pies are also well-loved sloe recipes. The fruit is also used to dye clothes, such as linen, which initially is turned a reddish hue, washing out to a light blue.

Reports from the High Middle Ages in Europe between 1000AD and 1250AD document the sap of blackthorn, referred to as prunellier, being used to make writing ink.

The wood burns well, with negligible smoke. It polishes up well and makes good tool handles and walking sticks. In Ireland, the shillelagh is a cudgel made of blackthorn or oak. This weapon is also carried by officers of the Royal Irish Regiment as well as Irish Regiments across the Commonwealth.

Leaves are food for Lepidoptera larvae, (moths and butterflies) including the hawthorn moth, brown hairstreak, brown-tail, feathered thorn, brimstone moth, small eggar moth, Emperor moth, November moth, pale November moth, black and brown hairstreak butterflies, double square-spot moth and many others. Birds love to nest in the closely-packed, thorny thicket, feeding off the caterpillars and other insects, and enjoying the sloes in the autumn. The tree is susceptible to pocket plum gall, where the fruit elongates and grows without a stone.

Small Emerald Moth

The small emerald moth, or *Hemistola chrysoprasaria*, belongs to the Geometridae family. It is found throughout Europe to the Ural Mountains in Russia. It is also present in north Africa, Asia Minor and the eastern Asian mountains, including the Tian Shan, or Heavenly Mountains, in and around China.

The moth has a wingspan of 28 to 32mm. Wings are light green, fading with age to yellow-green then yellow-white. Two white lines form a continuous, slightly curved line across both wings.

The caterpillar feeds on old man's beard, *Clematis vitalba*, which grows at the edges of woods and hedges in the UK. Adult moths fly in one generation from June until August.

Small Tortoiseshell Butterfly

The small tortoiseshell butterfly is a familiar sight in Britain and Ireland, as well as Eurasia – wherever their larvae food of the common nettle and the dwarf nettle is abundant. This ranges as far afield as China, Siberia, the Himalayas, Mongolia and Japan.

Adults hibernate during winter, but are one of the first butterflies emerging in spring and will fly until late autumn. They have a wingspan of 50 to 56mm, and in warmer zones can have two broods a year. Although their upper wings are beautifully designed, their lower wings are dull, providing ample camouflage. They lay their eggs on the common nettle, which emerging caterpillars feed on.

Numbers are declining, but this is not due to lack of food. Factors such as air pollution, pesticide use and environmental decline have been cited. Global warming is also a concern, as these butterflies flourish in cooler, wetter summers. Brood size

Julia Johnson

is smaller in hotter conditions, as the nettle fodder has less nitrogen and water in its leaves and does not provide enough nutrition for the caterpillars.

Adult butterflies enjoy a nectar diet. They recognise food plants through aroma and colour. Their compound eyes pick up on both red and purple flowers – opposite ends of the colour spectrum. These flowers enjoy the pollination opportunities that the butterflies bring.

Hibernation occurs from late September, when the adults make their way to dark, protected places. They need to put on 20% of their body weight in fat, which makes them much slower, and therefore prone to attack by birds. Around half of all hibernating small tortoiseshell butterflies are eaten by rodents. These butterflies can cope with temperatures of -20°C.

The butterflies are well camouflaged from birds, which get distracted by their unusual markings. Their vivid red wings frighten their predators as it signals their unpleasant taste. They are pretty speedy butterflies and can overtake a bird if threatened.

Males will defend a territory for an hour and a half, mainly in the afternoon, after they have spent the morning feeding and basking in the sun. They are territorial as it increases mating possibilities, but can share territories if it gives them more energy for mating. Females tend to stay in dense groups.

Squirrel

The grey squirrel originated in the easterly parts of North America and was first documented in Carolina, hence its Latin name, *Sciurus carolinensis*. The generic name, *Sciurus*, refers to the squirrel's enormous tail, coming from the Greek words, *skia,* or tail and the *oura*, or shadow that it casts. The grey squirrel present in the UK is actually termed the eastern grey squirrel, as opposed to the western grey squirrel, *Sciurus griseus*, also found in the States. Although regarded as a pest in many of the countries that the eastern grey squirrel has been introduced to, including parts of western US, it is highly thought of in eastern US as a prime regenerator of native woodlands.

The squirrel has mostly grey fur with a white underbelly, and an exuberant, bristly tail, but can also be found in black, or even white, in some parts of North America, especially in urban areas where there is minimal risk of predation. Squirrels measure 23 to 30cm in length, with a tail almost doubling that, at 19 to 25cm. Both males and females share the same markings and weigh 400 to 600g. All species of squirrel have front feet exhibiting four toes, with five toes on each back foot. They are fast moving, with back feet overstretching the front feet in movement, and each pace measuring up to a metre long. They have 22 teeth, and like other rodents, have incisors that continue to grow throughout life.

Squirrels are remarkably clever when it comes to food. They hide their fodder in a multitude of small caches, which they retrieve at a later date, either to rebury or to eat. Sometimes they will leave these burial sites for months, and they are known to create thousands of hoards every year, using landmarks to remember where they put them. Although they do use their sense of smell to help re-find these important positions, this cannot be relied upon when the ground is too dry or covered by a layer of snow.

Occasionally, if a squirrel finds that it is being watched, they will mimic burying the food by creating a hole and covering it up again, whilst all the time secreting the food in their mouths. They like privacy when burying their hoard, often hiding behind plants or positioning it out of reach in the treetops.

There are very few mammals that can move down a tree headfirst. The squirrel is able to do this at speed, by positioning its rear feet so they face backwards and are able to secure a grip on the bark as they move down.

Grey squirrels create a nest, or drey, in tree forks or hollows, using dry leaves and twigs. Dreys are round and about 30 to 60cm in diameter. Squirrels will gather

feathers, dried grass, thistledown and moss to line the nest, and couples will sleep together throughout the breeding season and in very cold spells. However, they do not hibernate, and are crepuscular, meaning they are active both in the early hours of the morning and the late evening. They have a number of predators, including foxes, owls, domestic cats, hawks and weasels.

Grey squirrels are able to reproduce twice a year if there is sufficient food available. Younger females will probably only produce once a year, with the breeding season running from December to February and from May until June. Latitude, temperature and food supply all affect breeding success. If the first pregnancy fails, or the young are killed, the mother will conceive again in the later breeding period. Male squirrels compete for their female, and she will have multiple mates.

Litter size varies from one to four, with a gestation period of 44 days. Newborns weigh in the region of 13 to 18g and are pink and hairless. They are weaned at 10 weeks. Infant mortality is huge: only 25% of squirrels will see their first year, with around half of those dying the following year. From then, there is a 70% possibility of the squirrel surviving. Females are ready to start their own brood at a year old. Ovulation can be bought about by the presence of a male. Males begin to father at the age of one to two years. A squirrel can live to 12 years of age, although six is more common if they get through their early years.

A squirrel's diet is composed of tree bark, berries, tree buds, seed, nuts such as acorns, and various fungi. They are partial to eating the cambial tissue of sycamore and beech, causing lasting damage to the tree. They steal strawberries, corn and tomatoes. Squirrels also enjoy a diet of frogs, insects and small rodents, even occasionally eating their own species, as well as birds' eggs and chicks. They can be found gnawing on antlers and bones to increase their mineral content. They make the most of bird feeders in residential gardens, although in doing so, they prevent the wild bird population from accessing this food.

At the beginning of the twentieth century the grey squirrel was widely imported to Bermuda, Madeira, the Azores, Hawaii, Ireland, Italy, Cape Verde, the Canary Islands and South Africa. The United Kingdom saw its first grey squirrels in the 1870s, where they spread rapidly, displacing the native red squirrels which have all but vanished. Red squirrels are now only found in Scotland, in small populations in northern England and Wales and on islands of the south coast of England, for example the Isle of Wight. Diminishing numbers are still seen in Ireland.

Grey squirrels have the advantage over our native red squirrels in that they are larger, they can stockpile up to four times more fat, have larger litters, are able to weather the winters better and can live in higher densities. They also have the ability to kill the red squirrel as they carry the squirrelpox virus (or Parapoxvirus), which does not affect them, but has a catastrophic effect on the reds, nearly 25 times more deadly than any other competitive factor.

The other part of this equation is the low level of predation. The pine martin, no longer present in England and Wales, would have been a strong natural predator. The grey squirrel is regarded as a pest. Some celebrity chefs have even gone so far as suggesting we eat them, and the Native Americans certainly did. Some hunters in North America still do. The brains, however, should be avoided as there is the risk of Creutzfeldt–Jakob disease: an unusual neurological disorder that leads to dementia and eventually death.

Starling

The European starling, *Sturnus vulgaris*, belongs to the starling family, Sturnidae. There are twelve subspecies found across Europe and western Asia. The birds are resident in the warmer areas of this region, but will migrate in the north-easterly parts. In the UK, starlings are seen throughout the year, with migratory birds increasing numbers in the autumn and winter. They are found all over the UK, with the exception of the peaks of the Scottish Highlands, whilst the subspecies *S.v. zetlandicus* is present in the Shetland Isles and Outer Hebrides. The starling has been widely introduced across the world to countries such as Australia and New Zealand, Canada and the United States, Mexico, Argentina and Peru, as well as South Africa and Fiji. Numbers in the UK have declined due to the fall in numbers of grassland invertebrates that chicks need in order to survive; however, due to their wide range they are thought to be of 'least concern' by the IUCN.

Carl Linnaeus named the birds in 1758 in his *Systema Naturae*, using the Latin roots, 'common' and 'starling'.

Starlings are 21cm long, with a wingspan of 37 to 42cm and a weight of 75 to 90g. They have an iridescent black plumage, which has a purple/green sheen and is spotted occasionally with white. The female's underparts are more spotted than the males. They both have a yellow beak, but his has a blue/grey base. Juveniles are grey/brown. They have a relatively short tail, compared to other passerine birds. They also have strongly pointed wings and a waddling gait.

Passerine birds belong to the order Passeriformes, which makes up more than half of all bird species. Known as perching birds or songbirds, they can be differentiated by their foot structure, with three toes pointing forwards, and one facing backwards, aiding perching.

Male starlings are very vocal in the run up to the breeding season. Once they have found a mate they quieten down a bit. They sing for a minute or two at each burst and are expert mimics of other birds. Older starlings have a larger and more complex repertoire which makes them more attractive to a mate. Song is also used to communicate to the flock, for a threat, alarm or squabbling whilst foraging.

Starlings form huge flocks called 'murmurations', particularly in the autumn and winter near roosts. These are thought to act as a defence against raptors. The starlings fly in a close formation, changing speed and direction. They manage this by reacting to the movement of their nearest bird. Predators such as the northern goshawk,

Eurasian sparrowhawk, peregrine falcon and common kestrel are not agile enough to keep up with them. Starlings are able to fly up to 60 to 80km/hr. Owls prey on them as they roost at night, and the fledglings are caught by slower birds of prey, like the common buzzard and red kite. Squirrels can clamber into the nest to attack the chicks.

Roosts can sometimes be as large as 1.5 million birds. Droppings can be a problem, sometimes up to 30cm deep, killing trees and spreading fungal diseases.

Starlings enjoy a mainly insect diet, such as grasshoppers, spiders, beetles, ants and damsel flies. They also take small frogs, earthworms and snails. Grains, seeds, fruits and food waste are eaten too, usually by foraging from the ground. They exhibit roller feeding in large flocks, where the back row will fly to the front, to get the best grub.

At the beginning of the mating season, single male starlings find a cavity in a tree or building to build a nest. He uses plant material, twigs and straw, lining it with feathers and wool, sometimes decorated with flowers. Herbs, such as yarrow, give off a scent which helps attract a female. Males may mate with another female whilst the first is incubating the nest, although reproductive success is higher if he has just one mate. The female lays four to five glossy, pale blue eggs. Both parents incubate them for 13 days, with the female taking the night shift, as the male returns to the communal roost. The young are blind for nine days after birth, and are naked until seven days, when they develop a fluffy down. They fledge after three weeks,

but both parents continue to feed them for a further fortnight. Parents can bring up two to three broods each year. Only 20% of chicks survive to breed themselves. Starlings live about two to three years, although they have been known to live to 22 years in captivity. You cannot release the bird back into the wild once it has been domesticated as it will not survive.

There are thought to be 310 million starlings globally, with a territory covering nearly 9 million km². However, numbers have dropped in the UK by 68% from 1970 to 2007. This is thought to be as a result of changing agricultural practices; intensive farming diminishes the short grassland required by these birds to feed. The birds have been widely introduced globally because they eat agricultural pests, such as wireworms and the grass grub in New Zealand. Although the US realise the starling's ability to reduce insect pests, they consider the starling to be a pest species, out-competing local native species, such as the chickadee, nuthatch and purple martin. The starling exhibits such behaviour as eating fruit crops, digging up crop seeds and spreading weeds, causing $800 million of damage each year in the US. Although the starling is not so damaging to agriculture in other parts of the world, the IUCN has listed it as one of the world's top 100 worst invasive species. The US is home to more than 45%, or 140 million, of the world's starlings. They exterminated 1.7 million of these birds in 2008.

A flock of starlings was absorbed into the engines of an aircraft in Boston in 1960, killing 63 people.

Although starlings are massacred around the world, for example, in Spain where they are eaten, in the UK they are protected by law, under the Wildlife and Countryside Act, 1981. In 1949, a large number of birds landed on Big Ben, in London, causing the clock to stop. Attempts were made to net the birds, imitate their call and finally, use chemicals in order to draw them down. However, none of these efforts were successful.

Starlings are often used in the laboratory because they are so intelligent. Mozart had a pet starling. Its gift for mimicry allowed the bird to sing phrases from his work back to him.

Stoat

The stoat, *Mustela erminea*, native to Eurasia, crossed over to North America half a million years ago. The stoat is bigger than the least weasel and has a black tip on its tail. However, it is smaller than the native North American long-tailed weasel. Stoats were introduced to New Zealand in the late 1800s in order to curb the rabbit and hare population; however, they destroyed populations of indigenous, ground nesting birds.

The word 'stoat', is said to originate from the Dutch word *stout*, meaning 'naughty'. A group of stoats is called a pack or gang, with a male being known as a dog or jack, and a female being a jill.

The stoat is known as the weasel in Ireland, as Ireland lacks the least weasel.

The stoat's ancestors evolved five to seven million years ago, as grassland replaced forests. They originated from a larger carnivore, shrinking in accordance with their new food source. Both the stoat in Eurasia and the long-tailed weasel in North America developed about 2 million years ago, prospering in the Ice Age with their ability to hunt underground in burrows.

Stoats show a great difference in size between the genders, with male stoats measuring up to 32cm in length, whilst females are not more than 27cm. The tails vary too, with a male's tail being up to 12cm, whereas a female's measures up to 10cm. Males weigh an average of 260g and a female less than 180g. Both sexes have scent glands on their anus, cheeks, belly and flank, giving off a different smell to that of least weasels. The anus scent glands produce a heavy, musky odour when the stoat is threatened.

The stoat has both a summer and winter coat, moulting twice each year. In winter, fur will be dense and short, whilst the summer fur is bushier, but sparse. Stoats found in the north of their range will show a totally white coat with a black tipped tail throughout the winter. Moulting occurs as a response to light levels.

Males only produce sperm from May to August, and the female's heat is determined by day length. Her long gestation period of 300 days is a result of what is known as embryonic diapause, or delayed implantation into the uterus. So summer mating leads to new-borns in the spring. If the winter is particularly cold, the female can reabsorb her litter, but she can expect to spend her entire life in a state of pregnancy or heat. Kits are born deaf and blind, with a white-pink down. They are not able to thermo-regulate well, so huddle together for heat, weaning after 12 weeks. Their father takes no part in rearing them. Males take 10 months to become sexually mature,

THE SECRET LIFE OF AN ARABLE FIELD

whereas females are ready to mate at three weeks, before they have opened their eyes, and they often become pregnant before they have left the nest.

Male stoats have a territory, which encompasses the territory of several females. This is vigorously defended from other males. Territory size depends on the season, availability of food and mates. Older males have territories that can be 50 times larger than those of young male stoats. Their range is marked with urine, faeces and scent marking.

The stoat uses the nests of its rodent prey in which to live, lining it with the rodent's fur. These nest chambers are located in various spots, such as in tree roots, haystacks, rock piles and log piles. A stoat typically has many dens. Males and females do not share the same den.

Rodent prey is predominantly mice. The stoat attacks larger species than the least weasel, even those bigger than itself. It can take small birds and fish, climbing up into trees to locate a bird's nest. Very occasionally it feasts on lizards, amphibians and insects. Rabbits are a great source of nourishment, increasingly so, since the end of the myxomatosis epidemic. Young hares are also eaten. The stoat kills its prey with a bite to the neck, although larger animals, such as rabbits, are too big to die instantly, and often die of fright.

Historically, a stoat's winter coat was sought after by the fur trade, who used this ermine to trim the ceremonial robes of the House of Lords, and the academic gowns of Oxford and Cambridge Universities.

THE SECRET LIFE OF AN ARABLE FIELD

Stock Dove

The stock dove, *Columba oenas*, is a non-migratory bird belonging to the Columbidae family of doves and pigeons. The genus, *Columba*, contains the largest birds of the family with the biggest geographical range. Birds within this genus share similar characteristics of a pale grey/brown body, with white colouration on the neck and head, and a green/purple sheen throughout the neck and breast. The three species of pigeon in the *Columba* genus in the west of Europe are the wood pigeon, stock dove and rock pigeon, which is also known as the common pigeon. Numbers of the stock dove have increased by 54% in the UK between 1970 and 2007. It is however, the least widespread of all European pigeons.

The stock dove makes its nest in the hollow of mature oak or pine trees, in woodland, agricultural fields or parkland. Plantations of trees do not provide the necessary habitat. The bird has shown initiative, creating nests in old buildings, rabbit holes, poplar hedgerows, fissures in cliffs and quarries, ivy thickets and in the dense growth at the base of lime trees. It will breed in a nest box, but this needs to be large, with a depth of 80cm and a wide hole to allow the bird to enter.

Stock doves puff themselves out when courting, lowering their wings and fanning their tail. They pair for life, and the female lays two white eggs in a nest made from leaves or twigs. Both parents take it in turns to incubate them, with chicks hatching in 16 to 18 days.

Stock doves eat the new growth of plants such as buttercups, goosefoot and rape. They enjoy cereal grains and invertebrates. Depending on the habitat, birds consume acorns and pine seeds, also taking bay and hawthorn berries and a variety of beans and peas. They will come to the bird table.

The word 'stock' can cause confusion, with some thinking that the bird has been domesticated, hybridised and used as stock for sale and consumption. However, the word, in this case, is from the Old English 'stocc', referring to a 'stump, post, stake, tree trunk or log'. Stock dove translates very literally into a 'dove that lives in hollow trees.' In the past, the trees known as stocc were gathered together for human use, which may have generated the word, 'stock', that we use today to refer to a supply of goods.

THE SECRET LIFE OF AN ARABLE FIELD

Sugar Beet

Sugar beet, *Beta vulgaris* subsp. *vulgaris*, belongs to the Amaranthaceae family of plants, together with other beet varieties such as beetroot and chard. It is high in sucrose and is the second biggest provider of white sugar globally, after sugarcane. The top sugar beet producers in 2016 were Russia, France, the US, Germany and Turkey, with Russia providing 51.4 million tons. The UK, that year, produced 5.7 million tons.

Although sugar beet was grown for cattle food, it wasn't until 1747 in Germany that sugar production started. The first sugar beet factory opened in Silesia, in modern Poland, sponsored by Frederick William III of Prussia. This caught Napoleon's interest in 1811, as the British were preventing the supply of sugarcane to France from the West Indies. He funded the foundation of sugar schools, giving them one million francs, and stopped imports from the Caribbean. Factories spread across the continent so that by 1880 it became the predominant source of sugar in Europe. Sugar beet was introduced to North America in 1830 and Chile in 1850. The US derives 55 to 60% of their sugar from this plant. In 2010, France was still the largest sugar beet producer in the world.

Sugar beet has a pale, fleshy taproot with an abundance of leaves above the surface. These leaves make sugar through photosynthesis, which collects in the root. Roots weigh 1 to 2kg, and consist mainly of water (75%), with 20% sugar, and the rest, pulp. Different cultivars have varying levels of sugar, from between 10 and 22%, with climate, soil, temperature and rainfall all having a bearing on this. After harvesting, the pulp is retained for animal feed, which gives the farmer an additional 10% income on his crop.

Sugar beet thrives in temperate zones, where it is grown throughout the summer. It has recently been cultivated in winter in warmer areas of South America, Africa and the Middle East. Seeds take approximately 10 days to germinate and 175 to 200 days to harvest. The highest sugar levels are found when the crop has warm weather, followed up by a cooler period. Ideally, rain levels of 610mm are needed. Beets grown near the equator do not do so well, due to the short days and excessive heat.

Fertilisers are used throughout the growing period. Nitrogen is applied to allow the beet roots to gain weight, whilst slowing down maturation. Potash acts in the same way, but will cause a magnesium deficiency if too much is applied. Phosphate is not taken up so rapidly by the plant, but it adds to the size of the root, although hastening ripening. In the UK, harvesting occurs mid-autumn, and there is a need to hurry, as the soil might freeze if left too late. Crops are rotated with wheat or maize to prevent a build-up of root rots or nematodes, and as sugar beets tend to exhaust the soil, peas and beans can also be rotated with them to increase nitrogen content.

The fungus, black root rot, causes lesions on the stalk, whilst leaf spot, another fungus, creates yellowing leaves and a loss in root mass and sugar levels. Rhizomania, or 'root madness' is a condition where small roots grow from the tap root, making the plant financially unworkable. Worms, beetles and nematodes are also a risk to the crop. As a result, hybridisation has widely occurred to try and find new, disease resistant varieties.

Until the latter part of the twentieth century, beet used to be harvested by hand. Nowadays a root beater removes the leaf and crown, which are low in sugar. If the beets are left in the field for collection at a later date, straw is used to prevent frosting which causes the formation of undesired complex carbohydrates. The harvesting and processing period is known across the world as 'the campaign', with factories operating in the UK around the clock for about five months. The crop is checked for quantity of non-beet, as well as levels of sucrose and nitrogen in the beet. Payment to the farmer is determined by these factors.

The beet is washed and thinly sliced. It is passed through a diffuser, yielding raw juice and a pulp. The pulp is sold as animal feed, with a by-product of the process, vinasse, used for fertiliser or a growth substrate for yeast. A blend of calcium hydroxide in water, known as milk of lime, acts on the beet juice by removing impurities and preventing the sugar from crystallising. Thin juice is then created by adding carbon dioxide, which reacts with the lime, precipitating as calcium carbonate, or chalk. This thin juice is then evaporated to give thick juice. Recycled sugar is added to it, creating a syrupy liquid, which is further treated to give sugar and molasses.

Sugarcane production, as opposed to sugar beet, can use bone char, made from charring animal bones, or coal-based activated carbon. Beet sugar does not use this and may be more appealing to vegans and vegetarians for this reason. However, since there is a GM impact on beet sugar, (95% of crops in the US), many consumers prefer cane sugar. GM sugar finds favour amongst those who value an insect and herbicide free crop that is not so dependent on the weather, whilst others avoid GM due to health fears, such as antibiotic resistance, as well as allergies. The two sugars also taste different, with sugar beet more earthy, whilst sugarcane is sweeter. Sugar beet is crunchier, whilst cane sugar readily caramelises. Since both contain sucrose – a mixture of glucose and fructose, either sugar can cause diabetes, liver problems and heart disease, so the recommendation is not more than 6 teaspoons a day for women and 9 for men.

Sugar beet is used in the production of alcoholic beverages, such as rum or vodka. Molasses is spread on icy roads in North America as it lowers the working temperature of salt. There are plans in East Anglia in the UK, to use the surplus products of beet production to create biobutanol.

Sweet Chestnut

The sweet chestnut, *Castanea sativa*, is not to be confused with the horse chestnut, *Aesculus hippocastanum*. It also goes by the name Spanish chestnut, and belongs to the Fagaceae family of flowering trees and shrubs. It is indigenous to southern Europe and western Asia, where the edible seed has been used for centuries. Indeed, the term *sativa* is Latin for 'cultivated by humans'.

The tree grows to 20 to 35m, with a trunk diameter of 2m. They can live up to 1,000 years if farmed, but 500 to 600 years in the wild. They exhibit oblong-lanceolate leaves which can be up to 28cm in length, showing strong toothing. Their bark is deeply furrowed, twisting up the tree.

Sweet chestnut flowers contain both male and female parts. These 10 to 20cm catkins grow towards the end of June, with the female developing spiky capsules in autumn, containing three to seven brown nuts. These will drop in October. The plant cannot self-pollinate, but is anemophilous, i.e. it undergoes wind pollination, which reduces the effects of inbreeding. The nut contains two skins. Hidden within it is the creamy-white part for which it is cultivated, which forms from the cotyledon or embryonic leaf.

Trees will not generate seeds until they are 20 years old, although grafted cultivars can be productive from five years. Sweet chestnuts yield 30 to 100kg of fruit a year, between September and November. In 2006, the total world yield was 151,000 tons.

The tree needs a similar climate to viticulture, with 400 to 1,600mm of rain a year and average temperatures of 8°C to 15°C. Soil needs to be within a pH of 4.5 to 6, and the tree does not do well on clay due to its water retention. Before planting, seeds can be stratified, mimicking natural conditions, to temperatures of 2 to 3°C, allowing germination to occur 30 to 40 days later.

The tree is also cultivated for its wood. In the UK it is coppiced. The young wood is rich in tannins which makes it durable enough for outdoor use in fencing. This lightly coloured wood can also be employed to make furniture and roof beams. Balsamic vinegar is aged in sweet chestnut barrels, although the wood is not generally used in open fires as it spits.

Sweet chestnut seeds, gathered either by hand, or more expensively, with nets, are usually soaked in water for nine days which prevents the build-up of fungi or small worms. They are then stored in a high carbon dioxide environment which prevents the fruit hardening.

These seeds are traditionally roasted in their husks, or they can be peeled by scoring the nut and blanching it. They taste very sweet, and are added to poultry as a stuffing, as a vegetable or in nut roasts. They are used to make cakes, puddings, bread, as a soup thickener and for fattening stock, as well as acting as a coffee or cereal substitute.

The nuts contain a wide range of nutrients and are a good mineral source of copper, iron, magnesium, potassium and manganese. They can be eaten as part of a gluten-free diet, and are known to reduce coronary heart problems, celiac disease and cancer. However, care should be taken when cooking as their organic acid content is reduced by 15% through boiling and 50% after frying. Vitamin C levels lower by up to 50% when boiled, and up to 70% when roasted.

The sweet chestnut has a long history, surviving the last Ice Age in several areas in Syria and around the Black Sea. By 2100bc to 2050bc humans were beginning to spread the plant from its ranges in Greece and Bulgaria. The Ancient Greeks botanist Theophrastus wrote negatively about the medicinal value of the plant, saying it caused indigestion, but he did praise the attributes of its wood. The Romans continued this theme, utilising the wood in pier building and supporting structures that can be seen in archaeological sites dating from 100ad to 600ad. The Romans could have spread the sweet chestnut around their Empire, but evidence is scanty, although it is said that Roman soldiers ate chestnut porridge in the morning to strengthen them before combat. It is not until the Early Middle Ages that the tree really started making its way across Western Europe. Trees, several hundred years old, are found in the UK today, the oldest of which is said to be the sweet chestnut at Castle Leod, Strathpeffer, in Scotland. Records from the estate show that the tree was planted in 1550 by John Mackenzie, privy councillor to King James V and Mary, Queen of Scots.

The tree is a feeding station for many Lepidoptera species, with the case-bearer moth, *Coleophora anatipennella* and the rose chafer, *Macrodactylus subspinosus*, both feeding on leaves.

Sweet chestnuts suffer with fungal pathogens such as chestnut blight, *Cryphonectria parasitica*, and the ink disease created by *Phytophthora cambivora* and *P. cinnamomi*. This causes dark brown spots on the leaves and stem, initiated by mycelium infecting the root in humid conditions. Chestnut blight in the first half of the twentieth century destroyed a huge percentage of sweet chestnut trees across southern Europe and 3 to 4 billion trees in North America. Another threat, introduced from Asia, is the gall wasp, *Dryocosmus kuriphylus*. Biological controls have been implemented.

Teasel

The teasel, *Dipsacus fullonum*, is indigenous to Europe, Asia and north Africa. It has been introduced to other parts of the world, including North and South America, South Africa, Australia and New Zealand. It is an herbaceous biennial and can form a monoculture, taking over other vegetation in regions with a beneficial climate and lack of biological controls. In the US it is considered an invasive species, and although two parasitic moths have been tested in Slovakia in 2003–4, they have not been approved in the US, where they use herbicides instead. Teasel has travelled far afield due to impurities in crop seeds.

Teasels grow from 1 to 2.5m in height and display a spherical arrangement of purple, dark pink or lavender flowers. They start growing in a circle around the middle of the oval flower head, continuing in both directions, to the top and bottom, forming two narrow bands as the season progresses. Teasels have both prickly stems and leaves. The flowering unit is egg-shaped, between 4 to 10cm in length and 3 to 5cm wide. It is joined to the stem with a base layer of prickly, modified leaves. A single plant can produce up to 40 flower heads in July and August, each of which is capable

of developing over 800 seeds, meaning that 32,000 seeds can be produced each year, and enjoyed by wildlife. Once flowering is over, the head will remain, and the 4 to 6mm seeds are dispersed by water, animals, birds and humans.

The plant is thought to be slightly carnivorous, as discussed by Charles Darwin's son, Francis, in a paper to the Royal Society. Rainwater collects at the point where the spiny bracts join with the stem. The genus name, *Dipsacus*, comes from the Greek word, *dipsa*, meaning 'thirst for water'. This cup-like structure fills with water, stopping aphids and other sap-loving insects from reaching the blooms. These insects drown, and recent experimentation has shown that increasing the number of dead insects corresponds to a higher number of seeds. It does not, however, add to the height of the plant. These seeds are a valuable supply of winter food for birds, in particular the European goldfinch, and teasels can be grown intentionally to encourage their presence.

Fuller's teasel, the cultivated *Dipsacus sativus*, historically has been used in the textile industry in order to clean, position and raise the nap on materials, especially wool. The nap refers to the textured surface of a fabric, most obviously in velvets, corduroys and fleece, but also in silks and satins. During weaving, fibres stick out from the surface. Teasels would have been placed on spindles or wheels, teasing the threads. This practice continued until the late nineteenth century, when metal cards were used instead, but the teasel still has the benefit of breaking if the machine hits a snag, whilst the metal card would tear the fabric. The teasel gets its name from this ability to tease these fibres.

THE SECRET LIFE OF AN ARABLE FIELD

Thistle

Thistles generally belong to the Asteraceae family, and they exhibit sharp spikes on their leaf edges as a defence mechanism against plant-eating animals. They produce soft downy material, known as thistledown, which enables the plant to spread its seed using the wind. There are over 200 species of thistle worldwide, including 14 species in the UK, such as spear thistle, marsh thistle and cotton thistle (Scottish thistle). Tumbleweed is also classified as a thistle.

Most thistles are considered a weed, contaminating crops and downgrading pasture. Some species can be detrimental to animals, even if only a small amount is eaten. However, they are valuable for the bee population, creating sought-after monofloral honey (honey which has a distinctive flavour due to being made chiefly

from the nectar of one species of plant). Varieties of thistle in the genus, *Silybum* are grown for their seeds, which are used to make vegetable oil and medicinal products, such as Silibinin from milk thistle.

Many species of butterfly are attracted to the thistles, especially fritillary species. Gold finches are also a big fan of the seeds. The high levels of nectar present in the flowers make thistles particularly important for wildlife, with *Cirsium vulgare*, or bull thistle placed in the top three nectar producing flowers in the UK.

The thistle has long since held a special place in the hearts of the Scots. Alexander III of Scotland, who reigned from 1249 to 1286, made it their national emblem, and in 1470, during the time of James III, it embellished silver coins. Even today, the Order of the Thistle is the most noble chivalric order in Scotland, having been instigated in 1687 by James VII of Scotland/James II of England, who claimed it was a throwback to an earlier tradition. The thistle's significance, as legend tells, came about when an attacking Norse army were silently invading a Scottish camp in the dead of night, only to find that a shoeless Norse soldier stepped on the aforementioned plant and shouted out in agony. The Scots were awoken and the Norsemen lost their advantage, leading to the departure of the Norse from the Kingdom of Scotland.

Thrips

ost thrips are tiny, at 1mm long. Predatory thrips can be up to 14mm long. The thrip order *Thysanoptera* is divided into two major sub-orders, both of which are further differentiated into families. There are over 6,000 species, in 777 extant and 60 extinct genera. Most have feathery wings, which do not allow them to conventionally fly using the leading-edge vortex method. Instead they have clap and fling flight, using the available vortexes around them. They have unusual asymmetric mouthparts, using their left jawbone to cut into the plant. Saliva is formed and injected via a tube into the partially digested plant cells. This leads to a silver or bronze blemish on the leaf where they have been feeding. Thrips also cause leaf galls, where plant tissue becomes curled or folded. Some species create rosettes and horns in leaves.

Thrip eggs are 0.2mm in length. It takes them 8 to 15 days to reach adulthood, and they continue to live for about 45 days. They spend winter as eggs, larvae or adults in a state of suspended development known as diapause.

They are considered a pest by farmers as they act as vectors, transmitting plant diseases, although they redeem themselves by eating various insects and mites. Flower feeding thrips can be pollinators, with some biologists believing thrips were the first

species to act in this way, forming a symbiotic relationship with a particular plant over time. They tend to feed on new growth, such as buds, flowers and tender leaves.

Thrips from the Thripidae family are renowned for the damage they cause to onions, potatoes, tobacco and cotton. They feed on developing flowers and vegetables, leaving them discoloured and distorted and making them impossible to sell. Thrips are considered to be the quickest spreading invasive species globally, particularly as greenhouse farming becomes more prevalent. They develop a resistance to insecticides very quickly. However, the use of red light is shown to be effective at reducing thrip damage in melon crops in Japan. Biological controls, such as certain fungi, kill thrips at all stages of their life cycle. Soap spray, using domestic soap, is also shown to be effective. Thrips do not like water, and climb up the surface of the water to order to get away.

Thrips were first recorded in 1691, in a drawing by a Catholic priest. Linnaeus classified three species of thrip in 1746, also giving them their name. By 1836, over 41 species had been recorded. They are commonly known as thunderflies and cornfleas. Thrips can be dated back to the Mesozoic Era, 66 to 252 million years ago, where their ancestors fed on fungus.

Tree Sparrow

The Eurasian tree sparrow, *Passer montanus*, is found throughout temperate regions of Europe and Asia, south of latitude 68°N. They are resident in the UK, although some northerly populations in Europe do migrate. They were introduced to the US in 1870, where they became known as the German sparrow, to differentiate from the 'English' house sparrow and American tree sparrow.

In Asia, the tree sparrow is common in towns and cities, but in Europe it tends to enjoy the open countryside, dotted with trees. It has been affected by changes in farming practices in Europe, such as the increased use of herbicides and the loss of winter stubble, which significantly lower food resources, both of invertebrates and grain. Tree sparrows are thought to have declined by 93%, between 1970 and 2007 in the UK, although recent data suggests an increase. There are thought to be 20,000 breeding territories, mainly in the Midlands, southern and eastern England.

Both the male and female share a similar plumage, with a rich chestnut brown crown and nape, and black markings on white cheeks. Juvenile birds are slightly duller in colour. Tree sparrows are 10% smaller than the house sparrow, measuring 14cm long, with a wingspan of 20 to 22cm, and weighing 19 to 25g. The house sparrow is also easy to spot, with its grey crown. The two species sometimes hybridise.

Pairs can breed in isolation or form loose colonies. The male brings the nest material, a combination of hay, wool and grass, lined with feathers. The nest is built in a tree cavity, rock face, or in the roots of an overhanging bush such as gorse. Sometimes they will take over a disused magpie nest or that of a grey heron or black kite. She lays five to six pale grey spotted eggs, incubating them for two weeks, with two to three broods produced each year. The chicks reach sexual maturity by 12 months. They will use a nest box.

The tree sparrow's diet consists mainly of seed and grain, found by foraging on the ground, sometimes in the company of finches and buntings. During the breeding season, invertebrates, such as insects, woodlice, centipedes and spiders, will be taken for the chicks.

A tree sparrow will live for two to three years, although they have been known to reach 13 years of age. They face predation from birds of prey, predominantly from the sparrow hawk, but also from owls, falcons and the kestrel. Juveniles in the nest need to be concerned about attack from magpies, jays, weasels, rats and domestic cats. Like

other small birds, they are susceptible to disease and infection. Garden feeders can be host to many species of bird lice, as well as bacterial and viral infections.

Winter is a difficult time for the tree sparrow, due to limited food resources. The pecking order over who gets food in a flock is thought to be linked to the size of the male's black throat patch. The distance from the nest to the food source, particularly garden feeders, also affects feeding strategies due to fear of predation, with birds feeding less, with more scrounging and in smaller groups, in exposed settings.

Although the bird's Latin name, *P. montanus*, suggests a preference for mountain habitats, it is actually the German name, *Feldsperling*, meaning field sparrow, that is more appropriate. It has been found nesting at over 4,000 metres in Nepal, but this is atypical.

THE SECRET LIFE OF AN ARABLE FIELD

Turtle Dove

The European turtle dove, *Streptopelia turtur*, belongs to the dove and pigeon family, Columbidae. It is a migratory bird, arriving in the UK at the end of April/May, and leaving between July and September, overwintering in Africa. It is found throughout Europe and the Middle East, although rare within the north of this range.

Numbers in the UK have dropped dramatically since 1970, with an 89% fall in numbers to 2007. A study by the European Commission identified the various threats to this species as habitat loss or modification, drought and climate change, hunting and competition with other species, notably the collared dove. The parasite trichomonosis has also been recognised as a threat. Some 2 to 4 million birds are shot each year across the Mediterranean, in Greece, Spain, Italy, France, Cyprus and Malta, during their migration.

The turtle dove is a slender dove, smaller and browner than the collared dove, with chequered black, chestnut upperparts and a black and white neck patch. Both sexes have the same colouring. They are 26 to 28cm long, with a wingspan of 47 to 53cm,

weighing 130 to 180g, just a bit bigger than a blackbird. Juveniles are paler in colour, without the neck patch.

The turtle dove prefers open land to woodland, feeding on seeds on the ground. The nest is built in thorny species, such as brambles or hawthorn. Thin twiglets and roots are used to create a fine platform, sometimes stuffed with grass, rushes or hair. There are two clutches a year, each comprising two pink/white eggs. Both parents incubate these for a period of two weeks, and both feed the young a substance called 'pigeons' milk'. This is a soft, cheesy mixture produced by the crop lining – a muscular pouch in the bird's neck, which stores food and secretes milk. The young use their bills to remove the food from their parent's throat.

The Latin name *turtur* is thought to represent the sound the birds make in song. Turtle doves appear in the song *The Twelve Days of Christmas*, on the second day.

Wasp

Yellowjacket and hornet wasps are among the most well-known wasp species. They belong to the Vespidae family and are eusocial in that they have an advanced level of social organisation, with a single female producing the young which the non-reproductive workers care for. However, this is not typical for all wasps. Usually the females live and breed on their own.

Wasps have been alive since at least the Jurassic Period (145 to 201 million years ago). By the Cretaceous Period (66 to 145 million years ago) they had evolved into the super-families that exist today. They have diverged into more than 100,000 species. Wasps have successfully expanded all over the world, with the exception of the ice caps, ranging in size from the 5cm long Asian giant hornet, to the tiny chalcid wasp, which is 0.11mm in length.

Most wasp species are solitary. Only the Vespidae family contain social wasps. Their usual black and yellow colouring is an example of Müllerian mimicry, where two or more untasteful species, that share the same predators, will copy each other's defence mechanisms for the good of both. Wasps use their sting to protect against predators. They will sting a human if the person reacts to them aggressively. Although painful, the sting rarely poses a health threat, although in some cases it can cause anaphylactic shock.

Social wasps build their nests from plant fibre, such as wood pulp, which is chewed upon and weakened by saliva. Added to it are mud, plant resin and substances emitted by the wasp itself. A honeycomb nursery is constructed. Varying species will

nest in different places, but yellow jackets tend to aim for trees and shrubs. Other species nest in lofts or holes in the ground. Reproductive cycles vary with latitude, with temperate regions taking longer.

Wasps are made up of three body parts: the head, thorax and the abdomen. They have large compound eyes and mandibles for biting, but they also have a proboscis, which allows them to drink nectar. Wasps tend to avoid meat, instead sucking the body fluids from the species that they have killed. Larvae look like maggots and feed either from plant tissues or from other insect egg larvae that they have been deposited in. Adult wasps don't really need protein, as they don't live very long. Some species feed on secretions from their own larvae, which provides them with sugars and amino acids. In return they provide their larvae with insect food, which they need when they are growing.

Females are able to determine the sex of their offspring. The female can lay as many unfertilised eggs as she likes, and these will all develop into males. The queen needs these male drones to fertilise her and create female workers. Siblings are able to recognise each other by chemical smells, which stop them breeding together, thus creating a stronger gene pool.

Wasps are not generally known for their pollinating ability. They do not have the hairy bodies and pollen sacs of bees. However, mutualistic relationships have evolved over many millions of years; for example, *Agaonidae* wasps have developed in relationship with their host plant, the figs, with wasp fossils found in fig remains dating back 60 million years. With over 800 species of fig tree, each has co-evolved with a separate species of wasp to pollinate it.

Most solitary wasps behave as parasitoids, living in close alliance with their hosts, using their host's resources until the host dies. It is a slowed-down form of predation. Their exceptionally long ovipositors help in this. They lay the wasp eggs in or around the host, which stays alive, being fed on by the developing larvae. Other egg-laying devices include laying their eggs in another wasp species nest, where they either take the food meant for the other wasp larvae, or wait until the other larvae are big enough, and then eat them themselves.

The Ichneumonidae family of wasps caused Charles Darwin to doubt the likelihood of an all-loving Creator. He wrote in 1860: 'I own that I cannot see as plainly as others do, and as I should wish to do, evidence of design and beneficence on all sides of us. There seems to me too much misery in the world. I cannot persuade myself that a beneficent and omnipotent God would have designed the Ichneumonidae with the express intention of their feeding within the living bodies of caterpillars, or that a cat should play with a mouse.'

Some wasps are used as a biological control, starting in the 1920s in Brazil, to combat sugarcane borers. Although chemical pesticides took over there from the 1940s, interest was revived in the 1970s. The wasp species *Encarsia formosa* can be bought to control whitefly infestations in tomato and cucumber plants. Other wasps are cultivated to prey on aphids, such as the peach-potato aphid.

Weasel

The least weasel, *Mustela nivalis*, is the smallest member of the carnivorous Mustelidae family, which also comprises the polecat, stoat, ferret, mink, badger, otter and wolverine, among others. It is simply known as the weasel in the UK.

There is always some confusion about the difference between a weasel and a stoat. The weasel looks like a smaller replica of the stoat in the UK, although globally across their range they vary hugely in size. The weasel has a purely brown tail which is shorter and thicker, whereas the stoat's tail has a bushy black tip and is much longer – about half its body length. The stoat is the larger mammal, measuring up to 32cm in the body, whilst the weasel is smaller at 17 to 21cm, with a tail length of 3 to 5cm, and a weight of 55 to 130g. The other main contrast is their movement. Stoats bound across the ground, arching their back as they do so. The weasel, on the other hand, moves more quickly, with a straight back, scurrying along with its body flatter to the soil.

In Scotland, where there is more snow, stoats can exhibit a white winter coat, whilst the weasel remains brown throughout the year in the United Kingdom. They are both difficult to spot. The least weasel preys on rabbits, rodents (including voles and

mice) and birds. They are found throughout mainland Britain in areas of grassland, moorland, hedgerows, heaths and woodland. They can also be seen in towns and gardens. They like enough cover to protect them from their predators: foxes and birds of prey.

Female weasels are smaller than their male counterparts, both having a russet-brown coat with a white belly and throat. Their long, thin bodies allow them to chase their prey into burrows. They hunt day or night, all year round, even in the snow. Weasels also take poultry and are considered a pest, but they are extremely useful in keeping down the rodent population.

The name 'weasel' was originally used to describe the European form of the least weasel, but it has subsequently been adapted to cover other species in the genus *Mustela*, and is commonly used to refer to any member of this genus, of which there are 17 extant species. Indeed, 10 of them use the term 'weasel' in their common names. The least weasel is found throughout the UK, with the exception of Northern Ireland and most islands. The stoat, however, is found all over Ireland, where it is commonly called a weasel! The least weasel is found throughout Europe, North Africa, Asia and parts of North America and can live in altitudes of up to 3,000m.

Culturally, weasels have a reputation for bringing both good and ill fortune. In Macedonia a sighting of them is prized, whereas in Greece, they are seen as a symbol of bad luck. Japan has a long folklore regarding weasels.

Weasels will live for approximately two years. They are visible throughout the year. They are Britain's tiniest mammal carnivore and give birth twice annually, with three to six kits in each litter.

Wheat

Wheat is a type of grass harvested for its seed. Belonging to the genus *Triticum*, the most common wheat that is grown is *T. aestivum*.

Wheat is a huge international trade, making up a greater percentage than all other cultivated produce put together, with 730 million tons produced in 2017 globally, and set to rise. Rice and wheat are the most popular food crops in the world. Wheat takes up more land – some ½ billion acres. This magnitude is due to the range of climate and latitudes in which it prospers. As the Americas and Australia developed in the last two centuries, wheat production proliferated enormously.

Wheat was initially farmed in 9600BC in the Fertile Crescent region of the Middle East, spreading throughout Greece, Cyprus and the Indian subcontinent by 6500BC and into Germany and Spain by 5000BC. Britain and Scandinavia cultivated wheat from 3000BC, with Britain using it for thatching roofs in the Bronze Age, (around 2500BC to 800BC in the UK). China did not farm it until 2000BC. Egypt was the first country to bake bread in the heat of the sun, thereby creating a national food industry.

Wheat has been selected carefully by farmers over the centuries, and developments in agricultural machinery have exploded growth. The roots of the

plants are very deep, growing 2 metres into the soil. These roots, as well as the fructans stored in the stem, allow the plant to survive drought and disease. This is a useful function in countries with dry conditions, and for forthcoming climate change.

Wild grasses, for example rye, have been hybridised with wheat to create disease resistant strains. Gene sequencing of wheat has been a fascination amongst scientists for some time. They aim to increase grain production and biodiversity, as well as insect and disease resistance and ability to cope with stresses, such as varying amounts of minerals and moisture in the soil. The average global wheat yield was 8t/ha in 2018. The UK in that year was producing 16t/ha, with the record being held by New Zealand, who produced 17t/ha in 2017. UK initiatives aim to increase yields to 20t/ha in the next few years.

Wheat is self-pollinating. It is incredibly time-consuming to create hybrids, which therefore makes for an expensive seed. Wheat is defined by: its growing season, i.e. winter or spring; protein content (10% in soft wheats and 15% in hard wheats); gluten content, which determines its elasticity, (i.e. in rolling pasta); and colour of the grain, amber, red or white, as well as blue, yellow and black, all containing different levels of chemicals.

Wheat is used throughout the world, in bread, biscuits, cereals, beer, vodka, semolina, pasta, muffins and pies. 100g of wheat supplies at least 20% of the daily value of protein, manganese, dietary fibre, phosphorus, iron and niacin, as well as high levels of B vitamins and minerals. It contains 14% water, 70% carbohydrates and 1.5% fat, as well as 13% protein, of which at least 75% is gluten. The gluten present in the wheat has unique properties such as viscoelasticity and adhesivity. This allows dough to be kneaded and retain gas. White flour has less lysine in it, which is an essential amino acid.

For those at risk, gluten can cause coeliac disease, an autoimmune condition which affects about 1% of people in the developed world. Around 12% of people have a wheat allergy due to the gluten, which can cause neurological disorders, dermatitis and fibromyalgia. The plant contains proteins called amylase-trypsin inhibitors, or ATIs, which protect the plant against insects, but cause inflammation in the intestine in some people.

Farmers in Medieval England would save one quarter of their crop to use as seed for the following year. Due to improvements in nitrogen fertilisers, irrigation and seed selection, by the millennium, only 6% of the harvest was stored for seed. The use of fertiliser alone accounted for an increase in yield by a factor of 25. Rotation cropping systems with leguminous crops, used in Australia, have increased harvests by 25%. In dry areas, soil quality is maintained by leaving the stubble on the field. Irish farmers traditionally have very high yields, with Germany, the Netherlands and the UK also using high quantities of fertiliser. In parts of Africa and Asia, in conjunction with their growing economy, diets are becoming more westernised, leading to a preference for wheat products.

A crop takes 110 to 130 days to develop, with chemicals applied at precise stages of its growth. The plant is susceptible to various diseases, such as seed borne diseases, leaf and head blight problems, crown and root rot diseases, stem rust problems, and viral disease. Some of these can be controlled with disease resistant varieties and good farming practices, but losses do occur.

When it comes to pests, there are a variety of butterfly and moth species that feed on the plant as a larva. These include the flame moth, the setaceous Hebrew character and the turnip moth. Beetles and weevils create problems too. Rodents are also very fond of the crop, eating both newly shooting plants and mature grains, including those in storage, and with this ample feed, their population can explode.

White-Lipped Snail

The white-lipped snail, *Cepea hortensis*, is a common sight in damper regions of grassland, woodland, wasteland, hedgerows and gardens. It exhibits varying colouration but is recognised by the white band around its shell opening. It measures 16 to 22mm and can be seen all year round. It is similar to the brown-lipped snail, although smaller, and, as you would expect, characterised by a white lip to its shell, rather than brown. This shell is usually a yellowish-pink colour, sometimes reddish-brown, with five brown circles looping round its smooth, glossy exterior. The snail's body is grey, sometimes turning yellow towards its tail.

Given the choice, the white-lipped snail feeds on nettles, hogweed and ragwort. They are preyed on by birds and amphibians.

These snails have both male and female reproductive organs, but they need to mate so that they can inseminate the eggs that they each individually carry. There is a long breeding season, stretching from April to October, where each partner injects a 'love dart' of calcium carbonate into the flesh of the other. The mucus on the dart contains a hormone-like substance which enables more sperm to survive. Mating, and the exchange of sperm then commences. Once this is done, they hide their eggs in the ground. Each batch is made up of around 100 eggs, each measuring 2mm, and these take a month to develop. These eggs are a delicacy in some regions of the globe, known as 'snail' or white caviar. The resulting snails will have a soft shell, which enlarges and hardens as they get older.

Whitethroat

The whitethroat, *Sylvia communis*, is unusual in that it has seen a 5% increase in the UK between 1970 and 2007. It breeds throughout the UK, Europe and temperate Asia, migrating to Africa, Arabia and Pakistan for the winter.

This warbler shows sexual dimorphism, with both birds having brown backs and buff undersides, with reddish flight feathers. However, the male has a grey head and white throat, whilst the female has a brown head, and muddier throat.

The song itself is scratchy with a jolting rhythm, and a tone often described as 'scolding'. When threatened, it sounds like a Dartford warbler, with long, rough notes.

The whitethroat enjoys open farmland, nesting in bushes, small shrubs and brambles, eating insects and berries. It will lay three to seven eggs.

The genus name, *sylvia* is derived from the modern Latin name for woodland sprite.

Wild Marjoram

Wild Marjoram, *Origanum vulgare*, is known as oregano in Europe. It is native to Cyprus and Turkey and was used in Ancient Greece and Rome as an emblem of joy. The plant contains scents of pine and citrus and has many culinary applications. Other species of *Origanum* are also used in cooking, such as sweet marjoram and pot marjoram, the former of which hybridises readily with wild marjoram.

It is a perennial plant, with a height of 60cm, enjoying dry, infertile, alkaline soils, in chalk or limestone grassland, hedgerows, roadside verges and wasteland. It relies on seed dispersal for reproduction rather than vegetative growth.

The nectar produced by its flowers is utilised by bumblebees, butterflies and many other insects. Its oppositely arranged leaves are 5 to 15mm long and are shielded by a layer of tiny hairs. Flowers are minute and are seen from summer to the beginning of autumn. They are white to pinkish purple. The fruit is made up of four divisions called nutlets, each housing a single seed.

Wild marjoram is usually used as a dried herb, on pizzas, stews or with roasted vegetables. It can also be used in a dressing or sauce. The flowers and leaves can be frozen and added to a cold drink, and the leaves are used to make tea. Its oil is good to flavour food, due to the borneol, camphor and pinene content.

Medicinally, wild marjoram has uses for stomach problems and colds.

Although considered a tender perennial in the UK, it can be easily grown in the garden for culinary use, or in a wildlife garden, where bees and other pollinating insects aid seed formation.

Wood Mouse

The wood mouse, *Apodemus sylvaticus*, is a rodent in the family Muridae, and is found throughout Europe and northwest Africa. Also known as the long-tailed field mouse, it is Britain's most common mouse, living in grassland, heath and moorland, farmland and woodland, as well as making its way into towns and gardens. It has bigger ears and eyes in proportion to its size than the house mouse and is a darker brown in colour. It is 8 to 10cm in length, with a tail of 7 to 9cm, weighing 25g. It can expect to live for a year.

The wood mouse is a nocturnal animal, which may be an evolutionary response to predation. It is able to climb easily. It constructs nests out of plants, in underground burrows or in old birds' nests, otherwise inhabiting buildings during winter. Eating mainly seeds, such as those from the oak, beech, ash, hawthorn or lime, it takes them to the nest to stockpile. As seeds become scarcer, in the late spring and summer

months, it will eat small invertebrates such as snails and insects. Throughout autumn, it takes berries, fruits and fungi. Over the winter months, it attacks dormant bats.

Although nocturnal, a pregnant female may scavenge during the day to ensure that she has enough food. This mouse can shed the end of its tail if it is trapped, however it will not regrow. Wood mice do not hibernate, but they do become inactive in extremely cold weather.

These mice are preyed upon by many species, including snakes, weasels, owls and other birds of prey, foxes, household cats and dogs. Mice create their own small network of runs and nests in order to protect themselves. The tawny owl may restrain from breeding if there is not an ample supply of wood mice, as they rely so heavily on them for nutrition.

If there is a plentiful supply of food, breeding can take place all year round, but it is more usually seen between February and October, when multiple mating occurs. The gestation period spans 25 days, with four to eight young produced. Juveniles can look after themselves after three weeks of age and are mature enough to reproduce at two months. Each female has up to six litters a year.

THE SECRET LIFE OF AN ARABLE FIELD

Woodpigeon

The woodpigeon, *Columba palumbus*, belongs to the pigeon and dove family, Columbidae. *Columba*, Latin for pigeon or dove, is derived from the Ancient Greek word, 'kolumbos', meaning diver, signifying the movement of the bird whilst flying. The Old English name for dove is 'culfre', used from the fifth to mid-twelfth centuries. Middle English, in use from the mid-eleventh to late fifteenth centuries, further derived this word into 'culver', which has lent its name to pigeon-rearing areas, such as Culver Down on the Isle of Wight.

Woodpigeons are found throughout the year, i.e. they are resident in the UK, southern and western Europe. Those in the colder regions of Europe and western Asia migrate south in the winter. These birds are found in fields and woods and are a common sight in towns and cities. There are thought to be nearly 5.5 million breeding pairs in the UK, showing an increase of 125% from the years 1970 to 2007.

The woodpigeon is the largest and most commonly seen of all three UK pigeons, the others being the stock dove and rock pigeon. They are mainly grey with a pink

breast, white neck patch and white markings on the wings, seen clearly in the air. Woodpigeons are 40 to 42cm in length, with a wingspan of 75 to 80cm, and a weight of approximately 550g. Both sexes are alike.

The bird is known for the loud clattering of its wings when it takes off. It flies quickly, with regular wing beats. During courtship, the male will swell his neck, lower his wings and fan his tail. They are sociable birds, flocking when they are not breeding. They have a very recognisable coo-cooing call.

Woodpigeons build a thin platform nest of small twigs in a tree, whether it be in a city park or wood. The female produces two pure white eggs which she incubates for 18 days. Males will be quite territorial during this time, flapping their wings and leaping at intruders. Crows prey on the nests, especially earlier in the year, when the leaf cover is not so great. The young take 29 to 35 days to fledge, although if they are attacked, they are able to survive from about 21 days.

Woodpigeons enjoy a mostly vegetable diet, particularly cabbage crops, potatoes, turnips, Brussel sprouts, peas and grains. They will also take acorns, other nuts and berries, young shoots, seedlings, and occasionally ants and worms.

Although protected by the UK Wildlife and Countryside Act of 1981, the woodpigeon is considered an agricultural pest and is often shot, especially in parts of Europe where such legislation does not exist. However, in urban areas they are more trusting of humans.

Homing pigeons are domesticated and selectively bred from rock pigeons, and have the ability to find their way home over long distances. In competitive pigeon racing, distances of up to 1,800km have been travelled, with birds reaching speeds of 95km/h. Pigeon post is when these birds carry a message, which has been written on thin paper and inserted into a small tube which is attached to the pigeon's leg.

Yellow Wagtail

The western yellow wagtail, *Motacilla flava*, belongs to the wagtail family of birds, also containing the pipets and longclaws. They are found in the temperate regions of Europe and Asia. In Britain they are summer visitors, seen from April to September in open areas such as arable farmland, wet pastures and upland hay meadows, predominantly near a fresh water source. They winter to the south of the Sahara in Africa. Two other wagtails are found in the UK: the grey wagtail and the pied wagtail.

The Latin name, *Motacilla*, comes from the word *motare*, meaning 'to move about', and *flava* means golden-yellow.

The yellow wagtail is a small, elegant, yellow and green bird with a tail of moderate length and thin black legs. It is 17cm long with a wingspan of 25cm. The male performs complex courtship displays, quivering his wings whilst suspended over the female,

although they are more frequently seen hopping along the ground chasing insects. The male has very bright yellow underparts and face, with olive green feathering on top and brown/black wings. The female is similar to the male, but much duller in colour. Juveniles are paler still.

Yellow wagtails are similar to the grey wagtail, but can be told apart as the grey wagtail has a longer tail, grey upperparts and a greenish rump. Both exhibit the repeatedly wagging and snapping up and down of their tail, seen throughout their genus. This action flushes out insects. The yellow wagtail is a very cautious bird, feeding, but all the time watching for predators and confusing them as to the location of its nest. A yellow wagtail's diet consists of small insects, such as beetles and flies, and they are often found around the hooves of cattle and horses.

The cup-shaped nest, made of grass, plant stems and roots, is constructed in a hollow on the ground or in a tussock of grass. The female builds this, using wool or fur to line it. Around six eggs are produced in mid-May, which are light grey with buff spotting. The female sits on them for 11 to 14 days, and they fledge in a further 10 to 13 days. Both parents feed the young.

At present, there are 12 recognised subspecies, which differ in colouration throughout their range. The British subspecies *M.f. flavissima*, named by Blyth in 1834, is known as the yellow-crowned wagtail.

Ancient Egyptians record in the Pyramid Texts the importance of the yellow wagtail as a symbol of Atum, the first and most eminent Ancient Egyptian god. The yellow wagtail may even have been the earliest form of the Bennu bird, which took part in the creation of the world, and empowered Atum in his creative activities. The subspecies *M.f. pygmaea*, or Egyptian yellow wagtail, is resident throughout the Nile delta and the lower Nile.

There are thought to be 15,000 breeding territories in the UK, with an estimated 50,000 breeding pairs, although numbers have fallen by 80% since 1970.

Yellowhammer

The yellowhammer, *Emberiza citrinella*, is the most common member of the bunting family in Europe. They are resident across most of Eurasia, meaning that they don't migrate, although towards the east of this territory they travel up to 500km to warmer regions in the winter. Yellowhammers were introduced to New Zealand in 1862, by acclimatisation societies that specialised in introducing non-native species to parts of the world where it was hoped they would flourish. They have been very successful. Australia, South Africa and the Falkland Islands have also received imports.

These are colourful, little birds, with the male exhibiting a vibrant, yellow head, with yellow and brown streaks along his back feathers. His underbelly is also yellow and he possesses a chestnut rump. Females are duller in colour, and more streaked. Yellowhammers enjoy open ground, dotted with a few shrubs and trees; agricultural fields are perfect. Large flocks of yellowhammers, as well as other buntings and finches will form on fields outside of the breeding season. Their song is often indistinguishable from their close relations, the pine bunting of Asia, and the cirl bunting of southern Europe and North Africa.

The female builds a concealed nest, on, or close to the ground during the months of April and May. This cup-shaped structure is formed with grasses, moss and plant

stems. She lays three to five eggs, which are covered with an array of thin, dark lines, lending the bird the name 'scribble lark'. The eggs take 12 to 14 days to hatch, with the chicks ready to fledge within 11 to 13 days. Yellowhammers produce two to three clutches every year, requiring temperatures of 16 to 20°C in order to breed.

Predators of the young include rodents and members of the crow family (or corvids), such as ravens, rooks, magpies, jackdaws and jays. They destroy more than 60% of all nests. Adults are taken by birds of prey. Yellowhammers feed from the earth, although the change in agricultural practices and increased use of pesticides and fertilisers has created a severe decline in numbers in the UK. There has been a 57% drop in the years 1970 to 2007, with a similar picture across Western Europe. However, due to huge numbers found in the rest of its range, 54 to 94 million in Europe with the total including Asia at 73 to 186 million, and a range of 12.9 million square kilometres, the IUCN rates the bird as of 'least concern'.

The yellowhammer is host to 13 different flea species. It is shown that an infected male will not only create a smaller clutch of eggs, but will also be duller in colour, related to breeding fitness.

Two out of three subspecies of the yellowhammer are found in the UK. *E.c. citrinella* is resident in southeast England, whilst the rest of the UK and Ireland, (but not southeast England), are inhabited by *E.c. caliginosa*.

The Emberizidae family are made up of about 300 seed-eating birds. Linnaeus, the Swedish botanist, zoologist and physician, in his system of binomial nomenclature, first described the bird in 1758, giving it the Latin genus and species name that it currently holds. The term 'yellowhammer' was initially recorded in England in 1553 as 'yelambre', formed from the German word, 'ammer', meaning 'bunting'.

The bird's diet consists largely of seeds. They prefer starchy seeds to the oily seeds of brassicas. They enjoy nettles, docks, common chickweed, yarrow, knotgrass and cereal crops, preferring wheat and oats to barley. During the breeding season, a yellowhammer will consume more invertebrates to feed its young chicks, including grasshoppers, flies, caterpillars, earthworms, spiders and snails. After about three days, a greater proportion of seeds will be introduced into the chick's diet.

The yellowhammer is a large bunting, measuring 16cm in length. During the breeding season, both sexes exhibit a more vibrant plumage display. Moulting takes place after breeding, lasting around eight weeks. Males display a greater degree of yellow as they age. Young birds will moult shortly after fledging, to gain their adult plumage. They are ready to breed in a year, and partner for life. A yellowhammer lives on average for three years, although some adults in the UK have survived for 13 years. There is roughly a 50% chance that a juvenile will survive its first year.

Yellowhammers have developed regional dialects in their song, and mating usually occurs between those with a similar song. A male with a wide variety of songs is likely to be the most popular.